Rationalizing Acute Care Services

Pauline Mistry

Managing Director
Health Care Division
Oxford International Group

T0347483

Radcliffe Medical Press,
Oxford and New York

©1997 Pauline Mistry

Radcliffe Medical Press Ltd
18 Marcham Road, Abingdon, Oxon OX14 1AA, UK

Radcliffe Medical Press, Inc.
141 Fifth Avenue, New York, NY 10010, USA

British Library Cataloguing in Publication Data

A catalogue record for this book is available from the British Library.

ISBN 1 85775 125 6

Library of Congress Cataloging-in-Publication Data is available.

Typeset by Marksbury Multimedia Ltd, Midsomer Norton, Bath, UK
Printed and bound by Biddles Ltd, Guildford and King's Lynn

To
Matthew F McNulty Jr, ScD
Chancellor Emeritus, Georgetown University Medical Center

For his extensive contributions to health services management.

Contents

Preface

The management and financing of health care systems throughout the world is in a state of flux. Burgeoning demands for health care services resulting from greater awareness and higher expectations on the part of users as to the quality and timeliness of service provision; rapid technology change and capital intensity; as well as profound changes in demography are putting both public and private health care systems under considerable stress. In most developed countries expenditures on health care consume between 7–15 per cent of national income. Unless improved management and higher efficiency levels in the provision of health care services are achieved, present trends suggest that adequate and timely health care will become less and less affordable at the level of the individual, as well as societies. In some cases health care systems, unless radically changed, will break down.

Growing demand for health care comes at a time when governments confront dramatic resource constraints. With a squeeze on public budgets in virtually every country in the world, ways need to be found of de-linking health care from total dependence on government financing, in an acceptable manner. No civilized society can seriously contemplate the complete abdication of public responsibility for a basic level of health care; especially for the elderly, the infirm, and the poor. At the same time no society can ignore the fact that, with public preferences for much lower levels of direct and indirect taxation, more and more of the burden of paying for health care services will need to pass from the state to private families and individuals. That shift has major repercussions and implications for how health care resources are to be allocated and distributed, and how they are to be managed, so as to achieve an acceptable degree of convergence between growing expectations and actual delivery of services. This book attempts to focus on one aspect of that fundamental issue in the UK; the rationalization of acute care services.

The rationalization of acute care services is taking place all over the country and in many places is plagued with public opposition and misunderstanding. In the following chapters the need for rationalization is discussed in the context of the NHS reforms and a strategic thinking approach. The processes involved in any exercise in rationalization are outlined from the initial defining of the catchment population, planning service levels, determining costs and estate and capital implications, to handling public relations and public consultation, and dealing with future uncertainties such as policy changes accompanying a possible change in government.

The text is essential reading for managers and clinicians involved in acute care services, non-executive members of boards and trusts, and students of health services management.

If this book makes a small contribution towards an improved understanding of one of the major issues being faced in acute care services – the rationalization of services – it will have achieved its purpose.

Pauline Mistry
August 1996

1

Summary of changes in the NHS over the past decade

Introduction

In order to place the present rationalization of acute care services in perspective it is essential to understand the changes which have taken place in the National Health Service (NHS) over the past decade, and in particular the NHS reforms of 1990. This chapter describes these changes and their impact on the organization and current operation of the NHS.

For the first 41 years of its existence (1948–89), the NHS was centrally directed and managed. The reorganizations that did periodically take place were designed to improve the organization and management structures and not aimed at improving efficiency or financial performance. The first move in the direction of improved performance was the Griffiths Report of 1983. This introduced general management into the NHS in an attempt to respond to variations in efficiency and the lack of attention to quality.

Throughout the 1980s expenditure on the NHS grew in real terms, but the funding was not sufficient to meet the increasing needs of an ageing population and advances in medical technology. One of the most influential analyses of the NHS in the 1980s was made in 1985 by the American economist, Alain Enthoven[1]; he suggested that the pressures which faced the NHS were:

- the prospects for real growth in the level of resources devoted to the NHS were limited

- the NHS would continue to face pressures for increases in service levels due to demographic factors and the increasing costs of new medical technology

- the solution would be to improve the effectiveness of the service within the limited resources available; however, there were barriers to achieving this, namely:

  – a number of forces in the NHS – in particular its professional staff – made it difficult to bring about change

> – other than job satisfaction the system contained no incentives, for managers in particular, to deliver better quality care at lower cost. In fact it contained a number of perverse incentives whereby inefficiencies were rewarded by the allocation of greater resources.

The funding shortfall became particularly critical in 1987 and the greatest impact was on acute hospital services. Many district health authorities (DHAs) had to take actions such as closing wards and cancelling non-emergency admissions in order to stay within cash limits. It should be kept in mind that at this time hospitals were provided with fixed budgets regardless of the number of patients treated. Thus the most productive hospitals frequently ran out of funds as expenditures increased according to the number of patients treated.

In December 1987, following much adverse publicity associated with the impact of the funding shortfall, the government committed an additional £101 million to the NHS and the Prime Minister organized a broad review. The result of this review was the White Paper *Working for patients*, published in July 1989, and after consultation legislated through the NHS and Community Care Act of 1990, and made operational from 1 April 1991.

The 1990 NHS reforms

The main features of these reforms were:

- the separation of the purchaser and provider roles

- the creation of self-governing provider NHS trusts

- the transformation of district health authorities into purchasers of services

- the introduction of GP fundholding

- the introduction of contracts of service between purchasers and providers.

In summary, the reforms involved a transition from an integrated system of health services financing and delivery to a contracting system.

Underlying the reforms was the intent to challenge provider dominance and give greater attention to the needs of the patient and the public by introducing an element of competition into the system. Providers now had to compete with each other for contracts from purchasers, and district health authorities were allocated resources to buy services on behalf of the people living in their area.

The introduction of competition has encouraged providers to increase efficiency and to improve quality. The money follows the patient so income increases only in line with productivity. The separation of purchaser and provider roles evolved gradually over the first few years of implementation, but true competition could only be achieved if all units became trusts. As long as district health authorities were responsible for the financial solvency of their directly managed units, there was little incentive for them to move contracts from these units to other providers.

The first 57 NHS trusts were established in England on 1 April 1991. These included acute hospitals, community services, mental health, learning difficulties, ambulance services, and a combination of all these services. Whereas *Working for patients* had specified that trust status would only be available for acute hospitals with over 250 beds, it was quickly made clear that trust status was the preferred model. Accordingly a further 99 trusts were established in 1992, 136 in 1993, and by 1994 over 90 per cent of all services had trust status. On 1 April 1996 the last three directly managed acute care units achieved trust status.

Initially the performance of trusts was centrally monitored by the NHS Management Executive. This is now done by outposts of the NHS Executive, organized on a regional basis. Each outpost employs a small number of staff, the majority from financial backgrounds. The outposts are responsible for monitoring the financial performance of trusts, agreeing with them an external financing limit, and approving their annual business plans.

Alongside the district health authorities as purchasers are the GP fundholders (GPFHs). By April 1996 in England there were 3735 fundholding practices involving 13 423 GPs and covering 52 per cent of the population. To begin with, fundholding included a limited range of hospital services, drugs, and practice staff. In 1993 community services were added to include district nursing, health visiting, chiropody, dietetics, and some services for people with learning disabilities and mental illness. Gradually the number of elective procedures that fundholders can purchase has been increased, and as discussed later in this chapter, in April 1996 further changes were implemented to introduce three levels of fundholding.

The allocation of resources

Since 1991 funding has been allocated to district health authorities as purchasers of services on the basis of resident population; not, as before, to the providers on the basis of catchment population. Regional and district health authorities are allocated resources on a population-based formula, which from 1995–96 took account of:

- the age structure of the population

- health and socio-economic indicators from the 1991 census

- the higher costs of providing services in London and south-east England.

Initially the regional health authorities (RHAs) were responsible for making allocations to the district health authorities and family health services authorities (FHSAs). Since April 1996, when the regional health authorities were abolished, allocations are made directly to the purchasers from the NHS Executive.

Budgets for GP fundholders are set by the regional offices. Although there has been some progress on establishing benchmarks for allocations to GP fundholders, based on a weighted capitation type formula, budgets are still largely determined on the basis of historical level of activity for individual fundholders costed at local provider prices. Funds for GP fundholders are managed by the family health services authorities, but funding for hospital and community services is transferred from the district health authorities' weighted capitation allocations.

The impact of contracting for services

The types of service contracts are shown in Box 1.1. Initially all contracts were block contracts and the development of more realistic contracts has been hampered by weaknesses in both information and costing systems. Many purchasers were also reluctant to enter into more sophisticated contracts; block contracts provided the advantage from the purchaser's point of view of controlling expenditure. Most contracts are now of the cost and volume type.

Contracts with DHAs were initially priced on a cost per case basis by specialty, with only limited analysis at the sub-specialty and case mix level.

Box 1.1: Types of service contracts

Block contracts
The DHA or GPFH pays the hospital (or other provider) an annual fee in instalments for the provision of a range of services defined in terms of overall workload and costs. Small changes in the number of patients treated does not affect the cost of the contract.

Cost and volume contracts
Payment is guaranteed up to a percentage of contractual workload and, thereafter, made on the basis of actual numbers of patients treated.

Variable
Payment is made on a cost-per-case basis and is used to fund individual treatments outside the terms of a regular agreement. GPFHs make extensive use of this facility.

Extra contractual referrals (ECRs)
These are all treatments for which no contract has been agreed. DHAs keep a reserve to cover their cost and all emergency ECRs are paid automatically. Any consultant can refer a patient to another consultant without seeking prior permission of the DHA. Non-fundholding GPs need to seek approval from the DHA before referring patients out of the local area for non-emergency treatment.

Work is now ongoing to develop a common costing approach across the country based on health care resource groups. These are groups of procedures within a specialty which use a similar resource profile, and their development will facilitate cost comparisons between different provider units. Contracts with fundholders are costed and priced for the operative procedures they can currently purchase.

While quality standards are built into most contracts they are mostly non-clinical in nature. The most common ones are waiting times, patient satisfaction, and a requirement to undertake clinical audit.

The development of competition

The impact of competition has been felt most strongly in the major cities, particularly in London, due to the number of hospitals in close proximity to each other and all offering similar services. In addition, the introduction of weighted capitation at district level benefited the counties at the expense of inner cities, resulting in money moving away from expensive city hospitals to those in the suburbs with lower costs and greater accessibility. In October 1991 the government set up an inquiry into the future of health services in London, led by Professor Sir Bernard Tomlinson.

Outside of London these issues are being handled by health authority purchasers working with each other and providers to plan the reduction in acute hospital capacity which the market made inevitable. Major reviews of the future of acute care hospitals and health services have taken place, or are taking place, in most areas of the country.

In the 1970s and early 1980s the principal objective of health care reform was to contain expenditures. In the late 1980s and early 1990s the focus shifted to greater efficiency in the use of resources. This has resulted in what some writers call 'market management', in which the purchaser has a large role to play.

It should also be noted that the scope of competition varies greatly within the NHS. The reality in many parts of the country is a substantial purchaser faced with a substantial provider and with little alternative but to contract with that provider.

The move towards care in the community

At the same time as reforms to the NHS, the government introduced changes to the delivering and financing of community care. These reforms were intended to halt the rise in expenditure, remove the incentive to use residential care, and ensure that a wider range of services was available to those in need. The provisions were part of the NHS and Community Care Act of 1990. Local authorities were given the lead responsibility for community care and their role was that of enablers rather than direct service providers. Hence a community care market grew alongside the NHS market, based on a separation of purchaser and provider roles, and the use of contracts. These reforms were not implemented until 1993. A major role for the local authorities was the provision of an assessment of an individuals' needs for care. The local authorities were to employ care managers to work with GPs and other colleagues in the NHS to determine what services were required and then to fund such services.

There has been widespread concern as to the adequacy of the funding for this legislation. The community care reforms represent a shift from a funding system in which individuals were entitled to income support for residential care to one in which local authorities determine who obtains access to services by allocating a fixed budget.

From the NHS perspective, local authority funding shortages, assessment delays, and other weaknesses prevent the NHS from making the most cost-effective use of its scarce resources. Viewed from the local authority perspective the NHS reforms place burdens on community care through the pressure to discharge patients. The boundaries between acute and community care are shifting as care previously provided in acute hospitals is increasingly delivered in people's homes or community and primary care settings. The shift in the balance of acute sector provision is being made possible by developments in pharmacology, medical technology, anaesthesia, and minimal access surgery. Their influence is combining with cost improvement pressures to reduce lengths of stay, increase day surgery rates, and enable conditions to be managed outside of the traditional hospital setting.

The Health Authorities Act of 1995

The Health Authorities Act of 1995 was implemented on 1 April 1996 and makes changes to the overall organization of the NHS in an attempt to make substantial savings in administrative costs and take account of the devolution of responsibility. In 1994, NHS-led mergers reduced the number of regional health authorities from 14 to eight. The Health Authorities Act abolished the eight regional health authorities and replaced them with eight regional offices of the NHS Executive. These cover the same geographical areas but are much smaller organizations. It also established 105 health authorities formed by mergers of the existing 110 district health authorities and 90 family health services authorities. These mergers and streamlining, while aimed at making substantial reductions in NHS administration costs, are also expected to assist in cementing the concepts of seamless care between the primary and secondary sectors.

Although there has been no national requirement there has, in recent years, been a number of mergers between district health authorities. There has always been a wide variation in the size of health authorities and for the most part it is the smaller ones which have merged. (In 1992–93 the average health authority had a population of 395 500 and in 1994–95 the average population was 412 000.) Such mergers allow health authorities to achieve better purchasing leverage in the local health care market, although health authorities that merge can face difficulties in maintaining sensitivity to the different needs of small local communities. Health authority mergers are also likely to highlight duplication of services and lead to pressure for service closures and rationalization.

Towards a primary care-led NHS

In October 1994 the NHS Executive published the paper *Developing NHS purchasing and GP fundholding: towards a primary care-led NHS*. This paper emphasized the government's commitment to the concept of a primary care-led NHS, in which decisions about the purchasing and provision of health care are taken as close to patients as possible. Towards this end it announced an expansion of the GP fundholding scheme, described the role of the newly formed health authorities, and a stronger partnership between health authorities and GPs. In addition, from April 1995 the rules governing GP fundholder's use of savings were extended to include clinical audit, research and development, and training.

From April 1996 the expanded GP fundholding scheme established three levels of GP fundholding:

1   *Community fundholding.* For small practices with 3000+ patients, or for those not ready to take on standard fundholding. The scheme includes staff costs, drugs, diagnostic tests, and many community services but not acute hospital treatment.

2   *Standard fundholding.* The minimum list requirement has been reduced from 7000 to 5000 patients and the services which can be purchased include virtually all elective surgery and outpatient services (with very few high cost exceptions such as heart transplant and renal dialysis), and specialist nursing services, e.g. diabetic and stoma care.

3   *Total purchasing.* GPs in a locality purchase all hospital and community care for their patients, including A&E services. Four pilot projects are currently under way and a further 25 are being established. They will be evaluated to identify the most appropriate models for the future. Fundholders in a locality will normally form a purchasing consortium to spread financial risk and develop a purchasing plan in collaboration with the health authority.

Maternity services are being piloted in six standard fundholding practices as well as being included in the total purchasing pilots. Osteopathy, chiropractic, and patient transport services to the surgery are also being piloted within standard fundholding. Medical inpatients, mental illness, and other long-stay treatments are also to be piloted for inclusion at a later stage.

It is the government's intent that health authorities continue to have overall responsibility for working with GPs to ensure that the health needs of the whole community are identified and met. They will also continue to have a direct purchasing role on behalf of non-fundholding GPs and for services excluded from the fundholding schemes.

The health authorities have responsibility for assessing the health care needs of the local population and for developing integrated strategies for meeting these needs across primary and secondary care boundaries. Major elements of the health authorities' role include:

- *Developing strategy* – in collaboration with GPs, local people, local authorities, and other agencies to meet national and local priorities. They also remain responsible for public health functions.

- *Monitoring* – they advise on budget allocations to GP fundholders and monitor the way GPs fulfil their provider and purchaser role. They are responsible for ensuring that national policy and local strategy are implemented effectively.

- *Support* – they provide support to GPs through the provision of advice, investment, and training. They purchase direct those services which require a broad population base. They provide information to practices to support GP purchasing decisions.

As GP fundholding develops, health authorities will be expected to shift the balance of their activity towards these strategic, monitoring, and support roles. The health authorities are expected to understand and support primary care provision, to work closely with fundholders and enable GPs to become fund-holders, and to ensure all GPs contribute to the development of local strategy. The allocation of the main NHS functions as of 1 April 1996 are shown in Box 1.2.

Other government initiatives

In recent years two other government initiatives have made an impact on health service priorities: the *Health of the nation* White Paper and the Patient's Charter.

The health of the nation: a strategy for health in England

This White Paper, published in 1992, focused on five key areas which were selected on the bases of greatest need and greatest scope for making cost-effective improvements in the overall health of the country. The areas are:

- cancers
- coronary heart disease and stroke

Box 1.2: Allocation of NHS functions as of April 1996

NHS Executive (headquarters)

- Setting NHS strategic framework
- Securing and allocating resources
- Human resources management
- Working with clinical staff

- Performance management
- Developing and regulating the internal market
- Managing general medical services
- Supporting ministers

NHS Executive (regional offices)

- Ensuring compliance with the regulatory framework of the internal market
- Managing performance of purchasers and providers
- Disputes arbitration
- Approving GPFH applications and budgets
- Purchaser development
- Contributions to central work on policies and resources

Purchasers (DHAs/FHSAs)

- Implementing national health policy
- Assessing local health care needs
- Setting purchasing strategy for local needs
- Purchasing services for local needs
- Ensuring delivery to contract standards
- Primary care development
- Administration of GPs', dentists', opticians', and pharmacists' terms of service
- Patient registration

Trusts

- Providing services to purchasers' contracts
- Managing delivery to contract specification
- Meeting the terms of the 'established order' and mandatory financial duties

GP fundholders

- Purchasing services for patients
- Accountable to NHS Executive but day-to-day contact through health authorities

All GPs

- Providing primary care to patients
- Provision of diagnostic and nursing services

- HIV/AIDS and sexual health
- accidents
- mental health.

For each area the strategy sets out the overall objectives for improved health and a total of 27 specific targets to be met by set dates ranging from 1994 to 2010. Some of the targets are for changes in mortality, others are for changes in lifestyle which will positively affect individuals' health.

The strategic goal of improving health through *Health of the nation* was identified as a top objective for the NHS in the Secretary of State's *Priorities and planning guidance* for 1994–95, 1995–96 and 1996–97. This has ensured that the key areas and other White Paper objectives continue to remain at the top of the NHS agenda.

The strategy has an increasing influence on health commissions' plans to purchase services to meet the health care needs of local people. *Health of the nation* continues to remain at the top of the NHS management agenda as an overall strategy, reflected at all levels through local initiatives and contracts. The main focus of action in the NHS is in the health authorities, hospitals, community units, and primary health care teams, whose work ensures that commitments made in the regional corporate contracts are underpinned both by management action at local level and by suitable programmes.

The Department of Health has an ongoing programme for monitoring progress in meeting the *Health of the nation* targets and has established a number of working groups and task forces to advise and help in implementing improvements in each area. An annual report is published and widely circulated.

The Patient's Charter

The Citizen's Charter, launched by the government in 1991, introduced a set of initiatives to make public service more responsive to consumers. The Patient's Charter puts these principles into practice in the NHS. The initial 10 rights under the Charter are shown in Box 1.3. In January 1995 new rights, standards, and guarantees were launched; the main additional right is to be informed if you are to be admitted to a mixed-sex ward. New standards and guarantees include inpatient treatment, first outpatient appointments, emergency admissions, community care expectations, child admissions, and catering services. The Patient's Charter is very important to both providers and purchasers in setting the standard within which they must operate.

The trend towards mergers

Mergers or reconfigurations of services are currently a major feature of the NHS. Many of these mergers arise for local reasons rather than as part of a

---

Box 1.3: The Patient's Charter

The patient has the right to:

- receive health care on the basis of clinical need and regardless of ability to pay
- be registered with a GP
- receive emergency medical care at any time, through a GP or emergency ambulance service, and hospital accident and emergency departments
- be referred to a consultant acceptable to a patient when a GP thinks this is necessary, and to be referred for a second opinion if a patient and GP agree this is desirable
- be given a clear explanation of any treatment proposed, including any risks and alternatives
- have access to health records and to know that those working for the NHS are under a legal duty to keep their contents confidential
- choose whether or not to take part in medical research or medical student training
- be given detailed information on local health services, including quality standards and local waiting times
- be guaranteed admission for treatment by a specific date no later than 18 months from the date when a patient is placed on the waiting list
- have any complaint about NHS services investigated and to receive a full and prompt written reply from the Chief Executive or General Manager

---

national strategy. Mergers have occurred and are currently taking place at four levels: regional health authorities, district health authorities, FHSAs, and district health authorities and trusts.

As previously noted, the Health Authorities Act of 1995 abolished the traditional RHAs from 1 April 1996. In the two years prior to this the number of RHAs was halved by mergers and subsequently replaced by the much leaner NHS Executive regional offices. These mergers have been nationally driven on the basis of reducing the costs of managerial overheads.

During the first three years of the reforms there were about 25 trust mergers and as the health service and health service market change, these will probably increase. It is widely believed that trust numbers will be reduced by about 40 per cent over the next five years. The reasons for such mergers are varied and include increasing market share, cutting overheads by merging administrative functions, and recognizing an inability to continue as a single player. Mergers will eventually lead to rationalization of services as the new organization identifies areas of duplication and overlap in services provided from different sites and then seeks to rationalize them.

Trust mergers can have many advantages including stronger clinical services, an increased service base, more competitive services, economies of scale on both capital and labour, and the ability to rationalize the estate. On the negative side, mergers could mean a return to the old monopolies and the accompanying complacency.

A review of acute care hospital services in Leeds[2] has recommended merging the St James' and Seacroft University Teaching NHS Trust and the United Leeds Teaching Hospital Trust. This would create a trust worth over £600 million and one of the world's largest medical centres. The review has stated that the two trusts should be merged to form a single trust by April 1997, but there is substantial opposition from Labour MPs in the city. The two trusts have aggregate deficits of £14 million. The review points to 'unproductive rivalries' between the two trusts as a reason for their recommendation.

In December 1994 the NHS Executive issued operational guidance on provider mergers and joint ventures: *The operation of the NHS internal market: local freedoms national responsibilities*. This is discussed in more detail in Chapter 3.

Summary

A summary of the major changes taking place in the NHS since 1989 is shown in Box 1.4. This combination of changes has provided the background and impetus for the recent and ongoing rationalization of acute care services.

Box 1.4: Major changes in the NHS since 1989

1989	*Working for Patients* White Paper
1990	NHS and Community Care Act
1991	1 April: NHS reforms implemented
1991	The Patient's Charter
1992	*Health of the Nation* White Paper
1993	1 April: community care reforms implemented
1994	*Developing NHS Purchasing and GP Fundholding: Towards a Primary Care Led NHS* White Paper
1995	Health Authorities Act
1995–96	Allocation of resources on a population based formula
1996	1 April: Health Authorities Act implemented
1996	1 April: implementation of three levels of GP fundholding

---

References

1   Enthoven AC. (1985) *Reflections on the management of the NHS*. Nuffield Provincial Hospitals Trust.

2   Leeds Health Authority. (1996) *The Leeds review of acute hospital services: final report.*

2

The case for rationalization of acute care beds

Introduction

The health service reforms which came into effect on 1 April 1991 forced acute care providers and purchasers to concentrate more than ever on costs and efficiency. With limited resources available to purchase services, the higher the unit cost the fewer patients could be treated. Also for the first time in the history of the NHS the different components of such costs were being scrutinized, including the capital costs. Purchasers were beginning to realize that one way to cut contract costs was by rationalization of services. This, together with other major factors discussed in this chapter, made the need for change and rationalization of acute care beds both timely and essential.

At the NHS Trust Federation conference in September 1993, the then NHS Chief Executive, Sir Duncan Nichol, predicted: 'The decline of traditional hospital based acute care is set to accelerate dramatically over the next few years. The present organization of hospitals is still often wasteful and results in a spiral of acute costs. Too much is being spent on bricks and mortar.' In other words, the hospital bed as the major unit of currency of the NHS is losing value. In recent years there has been a shift in the pattern of illness towards more chronic, degenerative diseases which cannot be managed by inpatient care alone. At the same time there have been improvements in primary health care and community services, and advances in medical technology, allowing faster diagnoses and less invasive treatment. As a result the hospital bed is no longer predominant, but just one of a number of hospital and community-based resources used to provide integrated health care.

This chapter looks at the international scene in terms of rationalization of acute care services, the history of hospital growth and building in the UK, and examines the major reasons for the present trend towards rationalization.

The international scene

Throughout the developed world the number of hospital beds is declining. Some of this decline is occurring naturally, but in many places governments are forcing the pace in an effort to contain costs. The problems of hospitals being too small, in the wrong place, and with fragmented services, have long plagued older cities such as London. The solutions: closures, mergers, improved community and primary care services, often cause controversy and public protest. Nevertheless, the trend is likely to continue as can be seen from the examples below.

Germany: the number of hospital beds has declined from 700 000 to about 650 000 over the past 20 years.

Canada: in the province of Ontario nearly 8000 hospital beds were closed during 1989–90 as the health ministry tried to deal with funding problems.

USA: according to the American Hospital Association more than 400 hospitals in the USA were involved in mergers and consolidations between 1980 and 1991 and 353 hospitals closed between 1980 and 1988. In September 1994, New York City's Health and Hospital Corporation announced plans to lay off 3000 workers and close hundreds of beds. Behind the cut-backs are technological advances, shifting surgery to outpatient clinics, and the refusal of managed care companies to sign contracts with hospitals perceived as inefficient and thus more costly. Forty hospitals have closed in the past five years in the southern California area which includes Los Angeles.

Denmark: between 1981 and 1991 the number of beds was reduced by almost one third, and the reductions took place evenly across the country. Plans are now under way to merge the seven hospitals in Copenhagen into a single company under the leadership of the country's main university teaching hospital, Rigshospital. With 5200 beds it would account for a fifth of Danish capacity and create one of the biggest single hospital complexes in Europe. The aim is to introduce greater efficiency and to expand some activities such as heart surgery, which has a long waiting list. Some specialist departments are likely to be merged and casualty departments may be reduced.

Ireland: rationalization has closed five acute hospitals in Dublin since 1987; in addition, Dublin's Adelaide, Meath, and Children's Hospitals are closing and moving staff to a new shared site. In Northern Ireland the total number of beds has been reduced by almost a quarter in five years, from 14 154 in 1989–90 to 10 891 in 1994–95. Current rationalization is addressing overlaps between south Belfast's City Hospital and west Belfast's Royal Victoria Hospital.

Scotland: one third of hospital beds in Scotland were expected to be closed by the end of the decade. Under Scottish Office plans all hospitals were expected to achieve a 33 per cent reduction in acute beds by the year 2000. The biggest reductions are expected to take place in Glasgow and Edinburgh, though hospitals in other parts of the country will also be affected. In July 1996, this target was withdrawn by the Scottish Office in favour of locally determined reductions.

England: between 1990 and 1994 there were 245 hospital closures; of these 85 were psychiatric, 60 were geriatric, 60 were acute, and 14 were maternity units. A further 14 were specialist hospitals and 12 were unclassified.

The history of hospital growth and building in the UK

The existing structure of acute care hospitals is centred on the district general hospital. This structure results from the 1962 Hospital Plan, which sought to build a comprehensive hospital service to replace the uneven pattern of provision which the NHS had inherited at its inception.

In 1969 The Report of The Committee on the Functions of a District General Hospital argued that acute care services can be provided more efficiently and effectively by:

> *a comprehensive district general hospital rather than by a number of separate hospitals each with limited functions. Not merely can supporting services be more economically provided at one central site, but the patient who may be suffering from a combination of different conditions should not have to be referred from one hospital to another: he should ideally be able to obtain whatever hospital treatment he requires from a team of consultants working together in one district general hospital.*

This centralized provision of acute care services raised questions about access to services in terms of travelling time for patients, visitors, and hospital workers; and the provision of emergency services. Consequently, while many monolithic district general hospitals were built in the late 1960s and early 1970s, most of the towns and cities in which they were built still continued to maintain multiple hospital sites with services divided between sites (examples of this phenomena are Oxford, Sheffield, and Cardiff).

Major reasons for the rationalization of acute care beds

Since the 1962 Hospital Plan was published the work of the acute care hospital has changed radically. The majority of health districts around the country have been coping with the need for major changes in hospital organization and facilities for many years. Each area has a unique set of reasons for such changes, but many of the contributing factors are the same across districts. The major factors discussed in this chapter are the most common, but the list is not exclusive. They are:

- technological advances and changes in the mode of care
- the unsuitability of old buildings and high maintenance costs
- problems of inner cities and demographic shifts
- the shift to primary and community-based care
- financial pressures and competition
- changing health needs; the targeting of sections of the population with below average standards of health

- the provision of accident and emergency services

- medical staffing issues and the requirements of medical education and research.

Technological advances and changes in the modes of care

Acute care hospitals in all developed countries are experiencing the impact of technological advances in medical science and the resulting changes in the modes of health care delivery. Developments in diagnostic techniques, anaesthetics, and pain relief have greatly changed the experience of most patients and facilitated day surgery and shorter lengths of hospital stay. Changes in technology such as keyhole surgery and non-invasive techniques have decreased recovery time and reduced length of stay. There have also been major increases in minor surgery done in outpatient clinics and GP surgeries.

In September 1994 the Department of Health issued guidance on new priorities and targets to purchasers which specified that 50 per cent of elective surgery should be carried out as day cases. Many hospitals are now achieving and even exceeding this level and the NHS Executive expects to see health authorities achieving 60 per cent by 1996–97. The Royal College of Surgeons has recommended a wide range of surgical procedures for day case activity, and it is increasingly common for purchasers and providers to agree targets within contracts.

New drugs from pharmaceutical research will reduce the need for hospitalization and shorten inpatient stays, e.g. in the treatment of thrombolytics. As the emphasis on home based care and self-treatment increases, the drug companies are supporting the move with many new developments, for example, automatic pumps which inject specified volumes of drugs into a patient at prescribed times.

The number of acute hospital beds available in England has fallen from 158 000 in 1974 to 144 000 in 1982 and to 110 000 in 1993–94. The number of cases dealt with by day surgery has increased from 684 000 in 1982 to 2.1 million in 1993–94. The average length of stay in acute care hospitals has fallen from 8.6 days in 1982 to 5.5 days in 1992–93 and 5 days in 1995.

There remains a large national variation in the age/sex standardized beds used per 1000 population, as shown in Table 2.1 The scope for further cuts in bed numbers was revealed in a survey by the Audit Commission[1] which found that only half of the medical inpatients studied needed a doctor's attention; the rest were prevented from going home by a lack of community support.

As a result of the above changes and the way in which surgical services are supplied, there is a nationally falling demand for acute care hospital beds. As this process continues the remaining beds become more expensive for three major reasons:

1   the fixed costs of the hospital remain, but are spread over a declining number of inpatient episodes

Table 2.1:   Age/sex standardized beds used by the residents of cities in 1992–93

Area	Beds/1000	% difference from national average
Leeds	4.80	83
Newcastle	3.68	40
Manchester	3.52	34
Inner London	3.08	17
Liverpool	3.00	14
Birmingham	2.94	12
Bristol	2.81	7
All London	2.73	4
Outer London	2.51	−4
England	2.62	0

2   the patients admitted require proportionally more attention as they are more seriously ill

3   the real costs of capital assets means that they have to be fully utilized to earn the expected returns.

One way to check the relative growth in fixed costs is to increase the number of beds through hospital mergers and site rationalization.

The unsuitability of old buildings and high maintenance costs

Between 1990 and 1994 the NHS repair and maintenance backlog in England rose by 45 per cent to £2.2 billion. For the year ending 31 March 1995 this had risen to £2.32 billion. Part of the rise was attributable to a new element for meeting statutory and safety requirements since the lifting of crown immunity in April 1991 and part has been attributed to the 'major pieces of equipment' in hospitals built in the 1960s and 1970s starting to go wrong. For example, the Welsh Health Commission Services Agency revised its initial assessment for essential fire precautions at Cardiff Royal Infirmary from £15 million to £27.7 million; this was a factor in the decision to close the hospital and redevelop it as a neighbourhood hospital. It is expected that the NHS repair and maintenance backlog could be substantially reduced in the future by estate rationalization programmes across the country.

The number and type of buildings which will be needed in the future is currently open to question and is discussed further in other chapters of this book. A National Association of Health Authorities and Trusts (NAHAT) report[2] published in November 1993 argued that as few as 25 large scale, high technology centres could replace most of the UK's large acute units. The prognosis for the district general hospital concrete castles of the 1960s seems bleak. The report suggests that the bulk of services could be delivered from town or locality based units serving smaller populations than the traditional district general hospital.

The high technology centres could cover populations of up to two million while local hospitals would serve between 20 000 and 100 000. The message is very clear that equating the provisions of high quality health care with bed numbers is no longer valid.

Problems of inner cities and demographic shifts

As competition within the NHS has increased there has been a trend for purchasers outside of major cities to try to buy services from their local provider rather than send their patients to city facilities. This helps to support the local provider and keep them in business, is often favoured by patients as they are closer to home, and is facilitated by local providers offering services which at one time were only offered in larger teaching hospitals.

This phenomenon has been experienced by many cities. In October 1993, Birmingham changed its plans to build a £300 million mega medical centre at the Queen Elizabeth and Selly Oak Hospitals, in part because the health authorities outside of Birmingham were increasingly opting for more services in their own localities.

The introduction of the new capitation funding formula has tended to move funds away from the cities and to the counties, forcing may city purchasers to search for ways to reduce provider costs. In October 1993, Sheffield Health Authority announced that it would have to claw back £20 million over the next five years, meaning a major rationalization of services. Under the new formula, Sheffield lost 10 per cent of its annual funding.

West Sussex Health Authority (which was set up officially on 1 April 1995 when three health authorities merged), after years of seeing money go to London teaching hospitals, is finally heading towards its weighted capitation target with its 1995–96 allocation. West Sussex has been 9 per cent below its capitation target.

The shift to primary and community based care

The shift towards the provision of an increased volume and range of services in the community is already being felt by the acute care sector, although it is still far from the forecasted levels. Many factors have contributed to the current emphasis on care in the community. Chronic conditions are becoming more important in terms of case-load than acute illnesses, so that more care has to be provided on a continuing basis. Advances in medical and information technology are enabling investigations and treatment to be provided in a wider variety of clinical settings. Tight control on NHS expenditure will require providers and purchasers to consider the most cost effective way of providing services, including alternatives to hospital care.

In June 1994, NAHAT and the Welsh Association of Health Authorities and Trusts issued a report[3] into the results of their research into community based care. The report outlines the impact social and technological changes will have on the way in which medical services are delivered in the future. The pattern described in the report is of 'general health care teams' serving most of their community's needs, including health promotion, minor surgery, routine diagnosis, observation, and outpatient activity. Primary care teams will not just be a gateway to secondary care. The teams will form local clusters, the configuration of which will depend on the local circumstances varying between rural and urban settings, etc. The clusters will comprise local and peripatetic staff, and community hospitals.

The research project made a number of assumptions which were theoretically tested on sites in Powys, Neath/Port Talbot, and the Eastern Board of Northern Ireland. The sites all had different facilities and populations. The main proposals were that by the year 2002:

- health promotion targets would be met

- GP referrals to specialists would be reduced by 20 per cent

- each person aged over 85 would have a key worker

- 40 per cent of patient consultations would occur away from district general hospitals

- 80 per cent of surgery would be carried out on a minimal access basis

- 60 per cent of surgery would be day surgery

- acute beds would be reduced by 40 per cent

- each local community would have arrangements for NHS and local authorities to pool their funds to provide access to minor surgery, a minor accident service, therapy services, minor diagnostics, and social care.

The target of 40 per cent reduction in acute care beds was found tough to meet. The target that 60 per cent of surgery would be day surgery was found to be feasible for elective work but difficult for emergencies. While all these assumptions may not be totally achievable they do serve to illustrate the direction in which services are moving.

In all discussions on care in the community and a primary care-led NHS, caution must be exercised. As the London Health Economics Consortium point out in their paper[4] on hospitalization trends: '. . . available evidence suggests that in general and with the exception of some specific conditions, primary care is a complement to secondary care rather than a substitute for inpatient care. Its role as a substitute for outpatient care is, however, more clear'.

Financial pressures and competition

The NHS Executive's aim to equalize health authority funding by 1998–99 has varying implications for health authorities, with many large cities anticipating reductions in funding. This, together with the annual efficiency index requirements, has resulted in the need for many health authorities to examine the efficiency of their spending patterns. Unless they can make savings they will be unable to fund needed new services. From this perspective they will often consider reducing acute care beds and rationalizing services. As a result, purchasers often put pressure on their providers to reduce costs by rationalizing services such as reducing beds, moving from multiple to a single site, or even merging with another provider or trust. The current trend towards mergers at different levels has already been discussed in Chapter one. Examples of such purchaser pressure are shown in Box 2.1.

Changing health needs and the targeting of sections of the population with below average standards of health

There is still a very large variation in health levels between different regions and districts of the country and different groups within the population. The public health common data set for 1993 gives a variety of standardized mortality ratios (SMRs) which demonstrate these variations. For example, the SMR for all causes of death in the 16–64 age groups ranges from a high of 117 for the North West region to a low of 77 for South Thames. The highest value for ischaemic heart disease for all ages is 136 for Bury and Rochdale; and for lung cancer for all ages 164 for Liverpool. The lowest figures for lung cancer for all ages are 73 for Chichester and 66 for South West Surrey.

Meeting the targets of the *Health of the nation* is compelling health authorities to target areas of deprivation and address both social and

---

Box 2.1: Examples of purchaser pressure

In August 1995 the Oxfordshire Health Authority estimated that halving the county's eight trusts would save £2 million. The HA let it be known that it expected 'considerable price reductions from all trusts' in April 1996 through joint working and shared overheads, particularly from those facing cuts in income. Trusts have been warned not to cut services. At this stage it appears that the HA is not insisting on mergers, but is expecting sharing of some services, for example, information technology, personnel, estates, etc.

Shortly after the new North West Surrey Health Authority was established in May 1993 it initiated a review of local acute services by its two main providers, Ashford Hospital Trust and St Peter's Hospital, Chertsey. Three options were reviewed in great detail and related to moving acute services to one or other of the sites and closer collaboration between the trusts. Although it was found that a saving of £2 million to £2.9 million a year could be achieved by moving acute services to one site, there was very strong public resistance to changing the profile of either acute hospital to that of a community hospital. The local GPs favoured a merger of the two trusts with some service rationalization, but not the complete loss of acute services from one site. Finally, the HA recommended closer collaboration between the trusts as its chosen course of action. Consideration would be given to developing the concept of community hospitals, to addressing problems associated with junior doctors' hours, and to reducing management and support costs.

geographic access to health care. In some instances this will involve diverting funds from the acute care sector into primary health care, health education, and preventative care.

The provision of accident and emergency services

A national survey conducted by the IHSM in the spring of 1995[5] found that the changing nature of A&E services played a role in the reconfiguration of acute care services. There was a general recognition of the need to divide services into major trauma, minor injuries, and the care provided by ambulance paramedics. The Royal College of Surgeons 1988 Report on Trauma Services[6] demonstrates that outcome for major trauma is significantly altered by the status, facilities, and support services of the hospital to which the victim is taken. The provision of major trauma care necessitates a wide range of skills being available on the site including urgent interventions in neurosurgical and cardiothoracic surgical skills, imaging services including CT and MR scanning, and ITU and CCU facilities. The creation of such trauma centres will, of necessity, involve the movement of services between sites.

Consultant and other staffing shortages in specialties such as traumatology also bring into question the viability of smaller units. In January 1996 the government took the unprecedented step of permitting trusts to increase the number of staff grade doctors in A&E departments to assist with staffing shortages. The national ceiling on the number of staff grade doctors normally limits the number to one for every 10 consultants.

Medical staffing issues and the requirements of medical education and research

Medical staffing issues are increasingly forcing change. The implementation of the junior doctors' hours agreement has had a major impact on acute care trusts. The agreement stated that the maximum average contracted hours of duty of doctors in training by 31 December 1994 should not exceed:

- 72 hours a week for doctors working on-call rotas in hard-pressed posts

- 64 hours a week for doctors working on partial shifts

- 56 hours a week for doctors working on full shifts.

By July 1995, 96 per cent of the 27 600 junior doctors in England were in compliance with these targets for contracted hours.

In addition, postgraduate training requirements for minimum workload volumes in certain specialties are forcing rationalization and/or a move towards a consultant-led service. This concept of the direct relationship between the volume of procedures carried out and the successful outcome has long been recognized in the USA and other countries. Research evidence suggests that handling a high volume of work will achieve better outcomes in most surgery, cardiac catheterization, and trauma care, and may be of importance in other areas including neonatal care, burn care, and coronary care.

Larger specialty departments offered from a single site both facilitate medical cover and ensure larger volumes of each procedure. The fact that some patients will have to travel further for some services seems a small price to pay for a higher quality service.

The increase in emergency admissions

Despite the reductions in the length of stay and the move towards day surgery many hospitals are experiencing pressure on hospital beds due to a national rise in emergency admissions. Although the rate varies considerably across the country, 5–7 per cent per year seems to be the average increase over the past two years. As yet there is no conclusive explanation for the increase, although there is some evidence that it is supply driven; that is, as lengths of stay reduce, capacity is created, allowing more flexibility or 'leniancy' in the decision to admit.

Other studies have shown that the admissions procedure and, in particular, the seniority of the doctor who makes the decision to admit, has a bearing on the number of admissions; the more senior the doctor the less likely to admit. There are also questions over the referral patterns of GPs and whether some GPs are more inclined than others to refer patients to hospital, because they themselves are under increasing pressure or worried about liability.

A recent study conducted by the King's Fund and NHS Trust Federation[7] indicates that hospitals are treating more and more patients with chest-related and respiratory problems and that health authorities and trusts will have to develop ways of coping. The study rules out speculation that the increase was created by the growing number of elderly people, or GP fundholders referring more emergencies to conserve their own resources. It says that the bulk of referrals for chest pain and respiratory problems such as asthma are appropriate, contrary to initial theories. The report says that changes in the UK's climate, changes in GP referral behaviour in relation to chest pain treatment, and the availability of new drugs and technology also contribute to the increase. The report calls for 'systematic analysis' of the problem on a trust by trust basis. Such an analysis will be essential for all trusts involved in plans to reduce the number of acute care beds. Other factors identified in some areas as contributing to the increase include:

- some conditions or diseases previously treated at home are now referred to hospital because of new treatments

- the increase in the number of old people living alone means that if they fall ill there is no one to care for them and admission to an acute care hospital may be the only short-term option available

- both the increasing use and success of ambulance paramedics keep patients alive to be admitted

- greater health awareness and expectations on behalf of the public has lead to a quicker reaction to the onset of acute problems.

This increase in emergency admissions is being used by some critics of rationalization to call for a nationwide moratorium on the closure of acute care beds. However, it is suggested here that there are many avenues to explore and changes to be made before such action needs to be even considered.

Some GPs and health authorities are already looking at alternatives to emergency admissions. These include making better use of community hospitals or even nursing home beds for short-term nursing care supplemented by the GP. Another alternative now being developed in several parts of the country is to provide emergency, home based nursing care, where a community nurse can be put in a patient's home and/or make frequent visits while a clearer assessment is made of the patient's need. If such schemes are going to become widespread it is very important that they are first evaluated in terms of their clinical outcomes in order to ensure that patients are not denied the most appropriate care for their condition. Evaluation will also enable protocols to be developed in order to facilitate the most effective use of these alternative resources.

Trusts are also exploring options. Many trusts have found that establishing an acute medical intake ward can help to alleviate bed problems. Patients received prompt assessment and treatment on an appropriately staffed intake ward and should be redirected within 24 hours to the most appropriate ward for their continuing care. Some patients may be discharged to home from the unit and others to more appropriate community hospitals. Other trusts have organized a standby ward that they can open at short notice when bed pressures are severe. The overall objective of good practice in this area should be to accommodate the emergency admissions without having to cancel elective admissions or maintain excess capacity in the form of under-utilized beds.

The increase in hospitalization

It is essential that rationalization of acute care services is not confused with a decrease in services. As the London Health Economics Consortium study on the trends in hospitalization (op. cit.) has pointed out, despite reductions in acute care beds hospitalization has increased consistently since 1948, and increased significantly over the period 1982–92. In researching this trend they found that demographic change was not the most significant reason, nor were changes in the pattern of morbidity. In effect the loss of beds has been outstripped by major increases in daycase work and reductions in lengths of stay. These have more than compensated for the loss of beds and have effectively increased the supply of health care available.

The average number of inpatients treated over the course of a year in each acute hospital bed (the throughput) increased by almost 60 per cent between 1974 and 1988–89. This increased efficiency enabled more admissions to hospital (an increase of 23 per cent over the period), while the number of beds has fallen.

References

1   The Audit Commission. (1992) *Lying in wait*. HMSO.

2   NAHAT. (1993) *Reinventing health care – towards a new model.*

3   NAHAT. (1994) *Closer to home: health care in the 21st century.*

4   The London Health Economics Consortium. (1995) *Trends in hospitalization and the requirements for hospital beds: a review of the evidence.*

5   Turner J. (1995) *Current issues in acute care: reconfiguring acute care services II.* IHSM.

6   Royal College of Surgeons. (1988) *Report of the working party on the management of patients with major injuries.*

7   Harrison A, Hamblin R, Boyle S. (1995) *Analysing changes in emergency admissions.* NHS Trust Federation.

3

The future of the acute care hospital and the importance of strategic thinking

Introduction

At the present time there is much speculation about the future structure and organization of the acute care sector. This chapter describes some of the alternatives currently under discussion. Faced with this uncertainty and the range of different options under consideration, acute care hospital managers who are already having to cope with the major organizational changes of the past few years are often worried if the direction they are choosing for their organizations is the correct one.

Rationalization is not something which can be achieved overnight; once the plans are in place they may take several years to implement and usually involve large capital expenditures. Such plans, once implementation commences, cannot be easily reversed if they are found not to be in line with new national trends or policies, hence the importance of a strategic thinking approach as opposed to the old style of long-term planning. This chapter discusses the importance of strategic thinking and its role in developing acute care services appropriate for future needs.

NHS priorities and planning guidance

Every year the NHS Executive publishes key priorities for service development in the forthcoming year and over the medium term. In the publication for 1996–97 they list the six baseline requirements which purchasers are expected to meet annually and describe six national priorities for the medium term, i.e. three to five years. These national priorities will be supplemented by local priorities. The baseline requirements are:

- progress towards the *Health of the nation* targets
- Patient's Charter standards and guarantees

- waiting time targets and guarantees

- national and local efficiency targets

- agreed financial and activity targets

- control of drugs expenditure.

The medium term national priorities are:

- to work towards the development of a primary care-led NHS, in which decisions about the purchasing and provision of health care are taken as close to the patients as possible

- in partnership with local authorities, to purchase and monitor a comprehensive range of secure, residential, inpatient, and community services to enable people with mental illness to receive effective care and treatment in the most appropriate setting in accordance with their needs

- to improve the cost effectiveness of services throughout the NHS, and thereby secure the greatest health gain from the resources available, through formulating decisions on the basis of appropriate evidence about clinical effectiveness

- to give greater voice and influence to users of NHS services and their carers, in their own care, the development and definition of standards set for NHS services locally, and the development of NHS policy both locally and nationally

- to ensure, in collaboration with local authorities and other organizations, that integrated services are in place to meet needs for continuing health care and to allow elderly, disabled, or vulnerable people to be supported in the community

- to develop NHS organizations as good employers with particular reference to workforce planning, education and training, employment policy and practice, the development of teamwork, reward systems, staff utilization, and staff welfare.

These national priorities provide the framework within which purchasers and providers of services have to work over the next three to five years, and must be taken into account in any decisions which are made in relation to the provision of services.

The future organization and structure of acute care

For most of this century hospitals have been at the pinnacle of health care provision in the United Kingdom and all other developed countries. Today's hospitals have evolved from philanthropic institutions established to care for the sick poor, to complex, high technology yet labour intensive institutions with multimillion pound budgets.

At the present time there are many different scenarios for the future organization and structure of the acute care sector. However, there does appear to be consensus that there will be a diminishing need for acute inpatient facilities over the next decade, due to greater reliance on ambulatory and primary care, and community based services such as home care. As fewer patients are treated in acute care hospitals, the hospitalized patient of the future is likely to be older, sicker, and require more complex care. Some of the major factors which will govern the future organization of acute care are described below.

Future models for acute care

As already discussed in Chapter 2, a 1993 NAHAT report suggests that the best pattern of provision is one of high technology and trauma centres serving up to two million people and supported by town or community hospitals. The high technology centres would be characterized by expensive, advanced equipment. They would concentrate on highly specialized areas whose viability could only be sustained by a large catchment population.

South East Thames Regional Health Authority published a report in 1991[1] on the future of acute services and the Oxford Regional Health Authority published one in December 1992.[2] Both reports were based on the concept of the major high technology hospital, but with a much smaller catchment area than the NAHAT study, the South East Thames study recommending 300 000 and the Oxford study 500 000–800 000. The proposed size of the catchment population was probably influenced by the fact that NAHAT was looking to an ideal situation, while the two regions were looking at scenarios with their existing hospitals and sites in mind. All three studies are in agreement that:

- with increasing specialization it will not be feasible to provide for all types of care everywhere; as a result, larger regional centres will concentrate the skills and technology in one place

- small hospitals will provide a wide range of services with no loss of clinical quality; and that some services can be provided in smaller units such as health centres and GP surgeries.

There are several current trends which support these speculations:

- Royal College guidelines in areas such as A&E, paediatrics, ENT, vascular surgery, plastics, neurosurgery, neurology, and a number of other small specialties tend to promote specialist units serving larger populations

- sub-specialization and the need to make best use of some key clinical and nursing staff reinforce this trend

- in specialist surgery, paediatric intensive care, and major trauma there is evidence that units with a larger workload achieve better outcomes

- once certain specialties have been concentrated in particular hospitals, it may not be possible to sustain a full range of specialties in the remaining hospitals.

A primary care-led NHS

The main aims of the NHS Executive's proposals in their report *Developing NHS purchasing and GP fundholding: towards a primary care-led NHS* are to facilitate more GPs becoming fundholders, to ensure that decisions about purchasing involve GPs working closely with health authorities, and that health care decisions are taken as close to the patient as possible. GP fundholding is the perceived catalyst for change and innovation in the development of new types of service provision.

Primary care is being viewed as the focal point of the system, with GP fundholders playing a larger role as gatekeepers who control patient referrals and manage resources in an integrated system. This will shift the emphasis away from secondary care to primary care. Due to advances in medical and information technology, more surgery will be performed in ambulatory settings, e.g. laparoscopic cholecystectomy.

Over time it is envisaged that there will be an increased substitution of 'mid-level' personnel, e.g. nurse practitioners, to enable GPs to meet primary care needs. Medical technology will be more precise and simpler to operate, enabling it to be used in primary care settings, e.g. nurses carrying out endoscopies.

To manage the growing senior population, GPs and nurse practitioners will provide continuing care management of chronic illnesses, with increased coordination of community services such as home care and health visitors. Increased emphasis will be on health promotion to increase fitness and encourage healthy lifestyles.

Clinical effectiveness

It is also generally recognized that medical and surgical treatments will be subject to more rigorous tests of clinical effectiveness, which could reduce or eliminate some currently questionable or inappropriately used procedures such as D&Cs, gastric surgery for cancer, and surgery for the enlarged prostate. Such assessments of clinical effectiveness will result in practice guidelines and clinical protocols to maximize clinical efficiency and reduce resources by fewer procedures and hospitalizations.

Information technology

Changes in organization and structure will be supported by advances in information technology. Information technology in health care will become more user friendly and much more prevalent. Terminals or hand held devices will be available at all patient encounters whether at the hospital bedside or in the home. The eventual move to universal paper-less patient records will enable access to required data from any setting and immediate input of data into the patient record.

An integral part of the IT developments will be the NHS networking. In March 1995 the NHS signed contracts with British Telecom and Mercury for a wide area network. The network will carry telephone calls, computer data, and eventually images and other multimedia messages. The NHS Executive has set the target for 90 per cent of NHS organizations to be on the network by mid-1996.

Major issues to address

Whatever the ideal model, the form that health services take in different parts of the country will be shaped by the requirements of particular localities and the communities that live within them, as well as by existing investments in buildings and equipment. There will be many issues to address and resolve whichever of the above scenarios is adopted; these will include:

- most current purchasing authorities are small relative to the catchment areas proposed for the new super hospitals; they will have to combine purchasing plans if such institutions are to be built

- access to facilities will be a major issue, especially for the elderly and those without cars

- the new technologies will require new skills and will change existing professional boundaries with the hospitals

- medical education will need to have a stronger primary care focus

- changes in professional roles will need to be accepted; the traditional demarcations between the medical and nursing professions will blur as nurses develop new responsibilities as care managers for patients with chronic illnesses and are given increased areas of responsibility.

The Calman Report on cancer services

The consultative document *A policy framework for commissioning cancer services*, prepared by an expert advisory group on cancer and chaired by Dr Kenneth Calman, Chief Medical Officer of the Department of Health, was published in May 1994. The final report after consultation was published in May 1995. The report recommends a new structure for cancer services which basically follows the scenario for the future of the acute care hospital described earlier. Cancer services would be based on three levels of care as follows:

1   Primary care: this is seen as the focus of the care.

2   Designated cancer units: these will normally be part of a district general hospital with a full range of supportive services. These units should have a sufficient volume of work to provide secondary care for the more common cancers. The surgical management of cancer should be carried out by surgeons who specialize in a particular anatomical area. A lead clinician will be appointed to organize and coordinate the whole range of cancer services provided in the unit. In addition a non-surgical oncologist must be appointed for a minimum of five sessions per week and should also hold an appointment at the cancer centre. Nursing care for both inpatients and outpatients should be led by nurses who have had post-registration education in oncology.

3   The cancer centre: these will probably be part of a large regional general hospital which will provide a range of very specialized services, together with services for local patients with the more common cancers, in the same way as the cancer unit. The centre should deliver a full range of cancer treatment to encompass treatment programmes for less common and rare cancers and those treatment regimens which are too specialized, technically demanding, or capital intensive to be provided in the cancer unit. A small number of very rare cancers will be managed in a smaller number of cancer centres to ensure adequate specialization. It is recommended that these centres serve a population of at least one million. The centre will also have an important role in training, continuing medical education, and clinical audit for health care professionals. The balance of practice between the cancer units and cancer centres will vary in different regions, reflecting the distribution of the local populations, existing services, and local expertise.

The recommendations of this report probably mirror the way in which many clinical services will be delivered in the future. Namely, from highly specialized centres of excellence supported by less specialized and more locally available units which have very close links with primary care services.

The Calman Report has itself raised issues which are far beyond the provision of improved cancer services. The recommendations of the report appear to have widespread acceptance, yet there is no implementation plan or clear indication of where the responsibility for implementation lies. Virginia Bottomley, the Health Secretary at the time the report was finalized, noted that 'the recommendations cannot be achieved overnight' and did not promise any new funding to assist with the implementation. In many ways the report appears to put responsibility for implementation on the main purchasers, the health authorities. The major purchasers are expected to 'force the pace of change to the recommended centres and units in that they control the funds to pay for services'.

Overall the purchasers are being attributed responsibility in five areas where they are expected to build standards into the contracting process, namely:

- referral and diagnosis
- coordination between delivery at the three levels of care
- management of treatment
- outcome
- prevention and early diagnosis.

In the case of cancer services, dividing the providers into the appropriate units and centres should not be too difficult. In many areas the divisions from the purchaser's perspective will be fairly straightforward. In recent years many general hospitals have been developing general surgery into site specific clinics and most general surgeons now have so-called 'specific interests'. At the unit level there will need to be some movement of patients between units as patients will no longer be sent to hospitals which do not have a suitable volume of such cases. A greater problem for the units will be providing the appropriate consultant and nursing support and the support services. The proposed centres are also readily identifiable primarily in the major teaching hospitals; there may need to be some adjustments to ensure equal access in all parts of the country.

Responsibility for implementing the future structure

As in the case of the Calman Report the government seems to be looking to the purchasers and providers to shape the future structure of the NHS. They have laid the framework in terms of the NHS reforms and now they are *almost* sitting back and waiting for the market forces to work. In the report *The operation of the NHS internal market: local freedoms national responsibilities* the NHS Executive spells out the circumstances in which they, working with the relevant regional policy board member, will act to ensure the correct balance between local freedoms and national responsibilities. The guide stresses several principles:

- primary responsibility for the delivery of health services is delegated to trusts, health authorities, GP fundholders and GPs. The ground rules are not designed to restrain purchasers and providers, but to guide their actions
- there should be a presumption *against* intervention, to ensure the maximum freedom of individuals and organizations in using the system to bring benefits to patients. The NHS will intervene when it is necessary to protect the overall interests of patients or the taxpayer

- when intervention is necessary, the presumption is in favour of a competitive solution; the ground rules aim to promote competition as the sharpest way of providing incentives to efficiency and responsiveness.

The guide outlines four situations where NHS Executive intervention may be required:

- provider mergers and joint ventures

- purchaser mergers and boundary adjustments

- providers in difficulty

- collusion.

This puts the onus clearly on the managers in the health commissions, the hospitals, and the GP fundholders to plan and shape the course. This type of responsibility is very far removed from the traditional NHS style planning which managers have been accustomed to.

To survive and prosper in this environment 'strategic thinking' and 'vision' are required. Providers especially need to have vision of what the future NHS will look like and where their organization will fit in this very broad perspective. In this scenario managers have to plan in both a visionary and realistic way. There is no room for pie-in-the-sky dreaming; visions must be based upon a thorough knowledge of the organization and what can, in reality, be achieved.

The role of the acute care manager

It is clear from the foregoing discussion that the organization and structure of acute care is going to change and that change has already begun. It is also very clear that the government is looking to the purchasers to bring about these changes. This approach puts the acute care manager in a very tenuous position. His position is analogous to trying to operate a multimillion pound 'business' with the major customers making all the key decisions in terms of the products offered, the quality of products and volume produced, and the location of the organization. There are no examples of successful businesses which operate under these principles. In effect, it is beginning to look similar to the old days when the district health authorities ran the hospitals and there were designated 'regional specialties' to provide more complex care. In addition, with all the emphasis on public consultation, a cynical person may be forgiven for thinking that the general public could have more influence over the shape of things to come than the hospital manager. Adding to the manager's dilemma is the fact that while most acute care hospitals have in the past had one major purchaser, with the increase in GP fundholding and the onset of 'total fundholding' there will eventually be many more players in the game. To date the degree of future collaboration between these diverse purchasers is not known. If they end up all singing from different hymn sheets, how many tunes can a manager dance to?

In a truly competitive market the organizations which survive and prosper are those which provide the services or products which the consumer needs or wants, at an acceptable level of quality and at a fair price. This market position is achieved by the organizations' managers understanding the market, anticipating the needs, and gearing up their organization to provide them. In this respect acute care managers cannot afford to sit back and wait for the purchasers to run their show. They need to be proactive and not reactive if the NHS is going to survive and prosper.

It should also be noted that many purchasers are not fully prepared for the role that has been thrust upon them, and between purchasers there are wide variations in levels of competency. This variation between purchasers was illustrated in a study of health authority five-year strategy documents conducted by Sharon Redmayne.[3] A third of the strategy documents examined were found to be lacking in very basic information including an assessment of the existing service provision and an assessment of local health care needs. It is difficult to understand how realistic strategies can be developed without a detailed understanding of the current situation. This is another illustration of why the providers cannot leave it to the purchasers to set their course for the future.

The time is definitely ripe for acute care managers to chart the destiny of their own organizations in the interest of providing the public with the services they need and at the high level of quality they have in the past expected and are now beginning to demand. In the final analysis when a trust has to discontinue a service, close beds, or reduce the number of sites and make staff redundant, it is the hospital management which experiences the wrath of their employees and the general public, not the purchasers.

The case for strategic thinking

In many ways it is this type of external pressure to reorganize things that managers can often pre-empt by strategic thinking. They should have the ability to see the directions in which health care is moving and make their plans or develop their strategies within that framework. Given the direction indicated by the Calman Report on cancer services and many other similar directives, managers should now be thinking of all their other specialty services along the same lines; identifying their particular areas of strength and developing these, and maybe getting out of the services which they know they provide less well and for which some of their competitors are providing a better service.

The following two chapters describe some methods of analysing the needs of the population in the area and reviewing current services and assessing their strengths and weaknesses; but in the current environment managers should be thinking of evaluating their services on a regular audit type basis (possibly every two or three years). Aside from analysing patient data and ensuring clinical audit, thought should be given to major consultations with purchasers, all GPs, and renowned authorities in the specialty to get their assessment of the service. Such 'audits' can form the basis for planning the future of the service and for service developments.

In an article in the *Health Service Journal* in July 1994[4], Marie Thorne claimed 'Planning NHS-style may be dead', giving examples of how even the best plans and planning can be rendered inappropriate during environmental turbulence of the kind the NHS is currently facing. She goes on to say that 'Planning is no substitute for strategic thinking. Even worse, planning may stifle it'.

The book *The rise and fall of strategic planning* by Henry Mintzberg[5] is devoted to drawing out the distinction between strategic thinking and planning. Mintzberg points out that planning does not create strategy so much as programme a strategy once it is developed; planning gives order to vision. He characterizes planning as fundamentally a conservative process. Thus planning may promote change in the organization, but of a particular kind, change within the context of the organization's overall orientation. Mintzberg believes that planning breeds a basic inflexibility in organizations and so a resistance to significant change. He goes on to identify the following three characteristics of formally planned change:

1   it is incremental not quantum

2   it is generic not creative

3   it is short term not long term.

Finding a suitable definition for strategic thinking is much more difficult. Strategic thinking is basically a combination of vision, intuition, and expert knowledge of the business in question and its environment. In the words of Mintzberg:

Many of the great strategies are simply great visions, 'big pictures'. But the big picture is not there for the seeing in ring binders or financial statements. It must be constructed in fertile minds. And like all big pictures these are created from myriads of little details. Fed only abstractions managers can construct nothing but hazy images, poorly focused snap shots that clarify nothing.

To be effective, any organization has to combine analysis and intuition in its strategy making. In the words of Herbert Simon[6]:

The effective manager does not have the luxury of choosing between analytic and intuitive approaches to problems. Behaving like a manager means having command of the whole range of management skills and applying them as they become appropriate.

In order to begin to think strategically and have such vision a manager must have a great deal of knowledge about his own organization, the environment in which it is operating, and the 'competition'.

Obstacles to strategic thinking

There will always be in the environment what some management strategists have described as 'forecasting discontinuities', that is changes which are impossible to forecast. To a large degree the health service reforms of 1990 fall into this category; very few managers could have foreseen or imagined the extent of the changes to the structure of the NHS that this government legislation brought about. Neither can they predict with any accuracy what will happen in the next general election. We do, however, know that if there is a change of government in 1997 some changes in the current structure of the NHS and its operation can be expected. (Such changes are examined in more detail in Chapter 10.)

Health care is also an area which is greatly influenced by technological innovation. Again very few managers would have predicted the enormous impact which the recent developments in anaesthetics could have had on the whole *modus operandi* of health care delivery, in terms of day surgery and shorter lengths of stay, or the developments in radiology which have revolutionized both diagnoses and treatment of many conditions.

To be successful in the health care 'business' of the future managers need to keep abreast of ongoing research and what the possible impact on the delivery system could be. The most obvious case in point at the present time is in the area of genetic engineering and the potential impact of developments in this field on the elimination of diseases, which currently consume a lot of the available resources.

The information required to support strategic thinking

While strategic thinking involves a degree of 'vision' and 'creativity', to be effective it has, like the more traditional planning, to be based on a great deal of detailed knowledge of the population to be served and the current patient activity of the organization. In either case it is not sufficient to think one knows the population in the catchment area or to 'have a feel for' what the organization is doing in each service area; factual information is essential and such information must be constantly updated. The next two chapters describe the minimum information required in these areas.

References

1   South East Thames Regional Health Authority. (1991) *Shaping the future: a review of acute services.*

2   Dixon PN, Gatherer A, Pollock RM. (1992) *Hospital services for the 21st century.* Oxford Regional Health Authority.

3   Redmayne S. (1995) *Reshaping the NHS: strategies, priorities and resource allocation.* NAHAT Research Paper No. 16.

4   Thorne M. (1994) Go with the flow. *Health Service Journal.* **104**(5413):33.

5   Mintzberg H. (1994) *The rise and fall of strategic planning.* Prentice-Hall.

6   Simon HA. (1987) *Making management decisions: the role of intuition and emotion.* Academy of Management Executive.

4

Understanding the catchment population

Introduction

Under the theoretical concept of health services planning and prior to the NHS reforms, the number of beds and range of services offered by a district general hospital should have reflected the health care needs of the population in the hospital catchment area and those of population groups from other areas in close proximity for which the hospital may offer specialized services (i.e. the old concept of 'regional specialties'). In the new environment of competition, the internal market and the projected differentiation of various levels of specialty services into regional, district and community services, this may not necessarily be the case.

The prior three chapters have described the developments in the NHS over the past decade, the rationale for fewer acute care beds, and the need for 'strategic thinking' as opposed to the old style planning on the part of managers of acute care facilities. As discussed in Chapter 1, the NHS Executive has charged the newly formed health authorities with the responsibility for assessing the health care needs of the local population and for developing integrated strategies for meeting these needs through their purchasing plans and those of the GP fundholders in their areas. Various NHS reports and initiatives in different specialties are forecasting a restructuring of acute care services on three levels: regional centres of excellence, smaller supporting district facilities, and a base of community hospitals.

It is the theme of this text that if the managers of acute care facilities are to be the masters of their own destinies, they must chart their own course in terms of determining what type of facility is most appropriate for their organization in the future structure of the NHS and which services they want and need to provide, as opposed to waiting for the health authorities or GP fundholders to plan their services by telling them what they wish to purchase. While these decisions can be arrived at through the strategic thinking process, effective strategic thinking can only take place if there is a thorough understanding of the population to be served, their health care needs, the current capability of the organization to meet these needs, and what must be accomplished to ensure such needs are met. Therefore, while it may be the responsibility of the health authority to assess health care needs, the providers also need to have a thorough understanding of the population and their health care needs so that they can plan the appropriate services. For example, while the concept of the general hospital is to provide a wide range of services, a hospital in an area populated primarily by elderly persons will need to concentrate on the type of health care services needed by this group such as geriatric medicine, general medicine, and orthopaedics rather than providing excess services in obstetrics or paediatrics, etc. It is essential to know and understand the population the hospital is caring for in terms of the factors which will effect their need for health care services. Such factors will include: population size, age, sex, ethnic origin, education, and economic status.

Defining the catchment area

Before any specific data on the catchment population can be collected the 'catchment area' of the hospital must be identified and specified. In the case of some hospitals this will be very obvious and straightforward, but in other instances it will be more difficult to define. The more obvious cases are those where the hospital (or group of hospitals) is the only provider in a geographic area, so to travel to another facility would be difficult for the patient. One example of this is the Cornwall peninsula. The more difficult cases are those of city hospitals, where the hospitals may be in close geographical proximity and offering the same range of services, such as the London hospitals.

While most consultants and hospital managers will have a good idea of where their patients are coming from, patterns of referral can change, particularly in the present competitive environment and with the increase in GP fundholding; also, perceptions can be wrong. Therefore it is essential to check the catchment area before embarking on an exercise of this nature and to set up the process to monitor it on a regular basis. (It is not sufficient just to look at the contract data in terms of purchasers and levels and types of service, as this does not provide a detailed picture of the population and sufficient information to project their needs.)

From a strategic perspective, any definition of the catchment area has two aspects, the actual area from which the patients are coming at the present time and the 'potential catchment area' or the area from which the hospital would like to attract more patients.

Verifying the catchment area

The most comprehensive way of checking where the patients are coming from is to analyse the patients' postcodes from the patient administration system

(PAS). (This is assuming that in the PAS all the patient data is postcoded.) Then by aggregating the postcodes for each district/locality (the post office can provide lists of postcodes for each district/locality or they can be looked up in the national *Postcode guide*) the volume of patients from different parts of the catchment area can be seen. Ideally, this should be done over the past three years in order to observe changes taking place.

The postcodes should be divided into inpatients, outpatients, and day cases for each specialty in order to facilitate further analysis. For example, it may be found that there are a large number of patients from a particular district across most specialties, but very few maternity cases although the district has a high proportion of women in their child-bearing years. There could be many different explanations for this: it may be further to another hospital but faster to get there owing to traffic patterns; the competing hospital may offer more modern facilities or organize services in a different way, etc. These are areas the hospital will have to investigate in more detail if it wishes to increase its maternity patients.

Another way to analyse this type of data is by the postcode of the patient's GP. This is interesting as it shows to some degree the referral patterns of GPs; however, in an inner city situation where GPs may be situated in close proximity to each other and if public transport is good or the population is affluent enough to have cars, they will often not choose the GP practice closest to their home. So using GP postcodes will not necessarily give enough information on the location of the patients.

Reviewing the population of the catchment area

Once the present catchment area has been defined and verified it is necessary to develop a detailed profile of its present and forecasted population. The most reliable source of population data is the Office of Population, Censuses and Surveys (OPCS). The OPCS produces data on the age and sex of the population broken down by county to district and then to electoral wards and civil parishes. (The data is derived from the census of the population conducted every 10 years; the most recent one took place in 1991 and the next will be in the year 2001.)

It should be noted that as of 1 April 1996, OPCS merged with the Central Statistical Office and the organization is now known as the Office of National Statistics.

Forecasts of the population are made by OPCS in five-year intervals up to 25 years and are available for both local authority and district health authority boundaries. (With mergers etc., many district health authority boundaries have changed or are changing; the latest OPCS forecasts are based on 1994 boundaries.) These forecasts should be compared with the current population figures, by age group and sex, to see the level of change expected. An example of this is shown in Table 4.1. From this example it can be seen that fairly large percentage increases in the over 75 years of age groups are forecasted for the

Table 4.1:   East Riding Health Authority: population projections (in thousands)

Age group	1995			2000			% Change from 1995	2005			% Change from 1995
	Male	Female	Total	Male	Female	Total		Male	Female	Total	
0–4	16.86	16.13	32.99	15.36	14.70	30.06	−8.88	14.63	13.99	28.62	−13.25
5–9	18.13	17.38	35.51	17.32	16.78	34.10	−3.97	15.81	15.32	31.13	−12.33
10–14	17.01	16.05	33.06	18.56	17.68	36.24	9.62	17.75	17.07	34.82	5.32
15–19	17.15	16.27	33.42	18.92	17.88	36.80	10.11	20.60	19.60	40.20	20.29
20–24	19.49	17.47	36.96	17.72	15.56	33.28	−9.96	19.53	17.08	36.61	−0.95
25–29	20.18	18.63	38.81	18.26	16.39	34.65	−10.72	16.59	14.58	31.17	−19.69
30–34	20.57	19.71	40.28	20.19	18.52	38.71	−3.90	18.22	16.26	34.48	−14.40
35–39	17.99	17.72	35.71	20.61	20.15	40.76	14.14	20.18	18.91	39.09	9.47
40–44	16.71	16.71	33.42	18.13	18.06	36.19	8.29	20.78	20.55	41.33	23.67
45–64	59.65	60.99	120.64	63.30	64.92	128.22	6.28	67.97	69.84	137.81	14.23
65–74	22.47	26.68	49.15	22.48	25.75	48.23	−1.87	23.40	26.15	49.55	0.81
75–84	10.69	17.83	28.52	12.41	18.94	31.35	9.92	13.75	19.91	33.66	18.02
85+	2.36	7.24	9.60	2.95	8.32	11.27	17.40	3.33	8.63	11.96	24.58
TOTAL	259.26	268.81	528.07	266.21	273.65	539.86		272.54	277.89	550.43	

Source: OPCS

next five- and 10-year periods. This should indicate to the hospital that the need for geriatric medicine and general medicine services will be increasing.

For health services planning purposes looking at forecasts for the next five and 10 years is generally sufficient. With the rapid changes in medical technology and modes of care it is not realistic to try to plan in detail for longer than 10 years. The highlights of the OPCS national projections for England and Wales are shown in Box 4.1.

OPCS provides a lot of other data on characteristics of the population which is useful in building up a general picture. This includes economic characteristics, ethnic origin, marital status, various characteristics of pensioners, household composition, dwellings, car ownership, etc. Some of the most useful data is listed in Box 4.2. Other characteristics such as levels of unemployment, single parenthood, numbers of dependents in single-carer households are also relevant to any analysis of health care provision and utilization.

Health characteristics of the population

Statistics on the general health of the population are also published by OPCS and readily available in many libraries, or can be purchased through Her Majesty's Stationery Office (HMSO). Most of the data is available by both regional and district health authority. Box 4.3 shows some of the information available and the frequency with which it is published.

Box 4.1: OPCS national projections for England and Wales: 1992-based

The population is projected to rise slowly from 51.3 million in 1992 to 55.5 million in 2027 and then to start to fall.

The main changes in the age structure of the population are:

- the number of children under 16 is projected to rise by about 5 per cent between 1992 and 2002, then to fall slowly until 2020

- the population of working age (males aged 16–64 and females 16–59) is projected to grow by 6 per cent over 20 years to a peak of 33.2 million in 2011 and then to fall by 5 per cent over the following 20 years. In this group the main increase is projected to be amongst those over 45

- the number of men over 65 and women over 60 is projected to increase by just 2 per cent between 1992 and 2001, and then to increase by 50 per cent to 14.8 million by the year 2032. The population aged 75 and over is projected to increase in line with present trends until about 2016 and then to rise more rapidly.

Although the population is in the short term thought to be ageing, this trend may be countered by immigration flows into the UK. Immigrants usually belong to younger age groups. Flows of new immigrants to some degree depend upon the world political situation and are difficult to predict.

Box 4.2: General characteristics of the population

Age distribution:	affects the patterns of mortality and morbidity, which vary considerably with different age groups; in addition it affects the rates of disability caused by acute and chronic diseases. Mortality rates and the causes of death are different for each age group. The same is true for morbidity and disability rates.
Ethnic and cultural:	some diseases are more prevalent in different ethnic communities. Such differences can also influence the outlook towards utilization of health care services, as can religious beliefs and teachings.
Economic status:	affects a population's ability to procure and utilize health services and to maintain healthy standards of living.
Level of education:	affects utilization of health services and influences approaches to the prevention of illness and accidents.
Household composition:	amongst other things this will indicate the number of elderly persons living alone, giving an indication of support services which may be required following a hospital discharge, or indicating a high rate of hospitalization because patients have no one in the home to care for them if they fall ill.
Car ownership:	is very useful information when planning location of services, especially outpatients. In areas of very low car ownership patient access to outpatient services requires particular attention.

By comparing the data in standardized mortality ratios (SMRs) one can easily see the areas in which health problems exist and consequently which services may need to be strengthened or emphasized. (The SMR is an index of mortality which recalculates the deaths in an area, as though it had the same age mix as a defined standard population, for example England and Wales. A value of an SMR that is less than 100 is better than the standard and a value greater than 100 is worse.)

Box 4.3: Health characteristics of the population

Information available	Frequency of publication
Birth statistics	annual
Legal abortions	annual
Deaths by cause	quarterly
Deaths from accidents and violence	quarterly
Infant and perinatal mortality	annual
Infectious diseases	quarterly

It is now essential for both purchasers and providers to take cognizance of their local performance in meeting the *Health of the nation* targets. As previously discussed, meeting these targets is a priority of the NHS and local performance should be closely monitored. In areas where targets are not being achieved, remedial action in the form of more or improved services must be planned.

Another source of information is the Health and Personal Social Services Statistics for England. These are published annually in November and provide a wide variety of information including hospital activity data by region and specialty. This publication is available from HMSO.

A potential source of information on the health of the local population will be the Annual Report from the Director of Public Health Medicine for the health commission. The quality of these reports vary throughout the country, but most of them will contain the most up-to-date information from OPCS on births, mortality and morbidity, and health status of the local population.

Health care needs assessment

While information about mortality and morbidity is essential for identifying relative health deficits, it does not automatically point to specific needs for particular services or other forms of intervention. To this end the type of data presented in the NHS Executive Needs Assessment (described below) is very useful, although it does only deal with a limited number of diseases or conditions.

In 1994 a series of epidemiologically based health care needs assessments was published as a part of the NHS Executive's district health authority project.[1] The aim was to assist purchasers by providing health needs assessments for diseases and services. The 1994 two volume publication contains the 20 topics shown in Box 4.4. The topics were chosen against the following criteria:

- the 'burden of disease', i.e. its mortality, morbidity, and cost implications for the NHS

- the likely scope for changing purchasing patterns in the future

- the use of a wide range of topic types to test the method used for needs assessment.

Each topic was prepared by a group of authors selected on the basis of academic expertise. The needs assessments were aimed at providing the major purchasers with the information they would require to purchase services for a particular disease. The diseases and services selected for review cover over one-third of health spending.

Each of the topics is addressed in a fairly standard format under the following headings:

- statement of the problem

Box 4.4: Health care needs assessment: topics included

Diabetes mellitus
Renal disease
Stroke
Lower respiratory disease
Coronary heart disease
Colorectal cancer
Cancer of the lung
Total hip replacement
Total knee replacement
Cataract surgery
Hernia repair
Varicose vein treatment
Prostatectomy for benign prostatic hyperplasia
Mental illness
Dementia
Alcohol misuse
Drug abuse
People with learning difficulties
Community child health services
Family planning, abortion and fertility services

- prevalence and incidence

- services available

- effectiveness of services

- a model of care

- outcome measures

- targets

- research priorities.

From such needs assessments both purchasers and providers can get some indication of the level of services needed now and in the future, effectiveness and cost of various treatments, and what outcome measures to use in service evaluation. By definition the data used in this publication is already a few years old, however the major information provided on each topic will be useful for many years to come.

For some diseases there are already widely accepted rates of the needs to be met. For example, a recent government-commissioned review recommended that health authorities should contract for 80 patients per million for dialysis programmes.

Planned changes in the area

In building a picture of the catchment population and reviewing population forecasts account must be taken of any major planned developments in the area which could affect the sex, age structure, or numbers of the population. Such developments could be the introduction of new industries which could mean a migration to the area and a population increase, conversely the closing of major industries could cause people to leave the area in search of work elsewhere. Construction of a motorway could mean the possibility of more high speed accident victims and an increase in demand for A&E and trauma services. Any such major changes will have an impact on the hospital. Such major planned changes are usually public knowledge and widely reported in the local press. The details can usually be determined by meeting with the local authority planning office.

Targeting populations outside of the catchment area

If the hospital has a specific service which it would like to market outside of its own catchment area, similar data as described above can be reviewed for different areas in order to identify the area with the population most likely to need the specific service.

Reference

1 Stevens A, Raftery J. (eds). (1994) *Health Care Needs Assessment*. Radcliffe Medical Press.

5

Analysis of current patient activity

Introduction

Before the number of beds and level of service required in future years can be projected it is essential that all aspects of the current levels of patient activity are known in detail. Understanding patient activity requires much more detailed information than looking at the number of finished consultant episodes (FCEs) in each specialty; it requires reviewing data from a variety of sources and over a period of time in order that trends can be identified. It also requires comparing the data with national data in order to identify areas where the hospital can improve efficiency, for example, by increasing rates of day surgery or reducing lengths of stay. This chapter discusses each of the areas which need to be examined as part of the analysis of patient activity levels.

Contracts with purchasers

The quickest way to get an indication of the overall level of patient activity is to look at the purchaser contracts. The contracts will provide the number of FCEs for most specialties and by looking at who the purchasers are, DHAs, GPFHs, and ECRs, a general picture of the level of service and main purchasers is readily available. Comparing contracts over several years gives information on changes in levels of service and trends. However, the use of contract data as a measure of patient activity is limited for the reasons described below.

A major problem with contract data is that it is in FCEs. Finished consultant episodes provide too general a picture for any detailed analysis. One FCE for the same procedure may be very different from another; for example, one FCE for a hip replacement may be an initial outpatient appointment, an eight-day length of stay and two follow-up visits, whilst another may be an initial outpatient appointment, a nine-day length of stay followed by a readmission for two days and four follow-up appointments. In other words, it gives no indication of the real level of resources and services being used. In addition, because the rules for identifying consultant transfers are variably interpreted and because local methods of handling transfers vary (particularly of emergency admissions), the number of consultant episodes within a hospital admission may vary.

An ongoing problem with using contract data is identifying case mix. In trying to understand patient activity it is essential to know what type of procedures are being carried out within each specialty. While the NHS Executive has stated that Healthcare Resource Groups (HRGs) should be costed and used by purchasers and providers to inform the process of developing contracts, an HRG may include procedures in different specialties. Although no standard contract is expected, purchasers and providers are expected to show that HRG costs have been used in the development of contracts and that the total price agreed is related to the volumes and mix of cases anticipated. Box 5.1 describes HRGs in more detail.

Contract data can also be used in analysing the competition. If the level and type of contracts let by the major purchasers to other providers are known a preliminary assessment can be made of 'the share' of the business in a particular specialty the hospital actually has. If the hospital is interested in increasing its level of service in a particular area, further analysis will then need to be carried out to determine how best to do this. As a part of this analysis the purchasers' strategies and plans for the next five years should be reviewed to give an indication of any future changes in purchasing patterns.

Box 5.1: Healthcare Resource Groups

Healthcare Resource Groups (HRGs) seek to assign cases to groups so as to reflect clinical and resource homogeneity. They seek to account for acute inpatient hospital work and are computed using software which reads hospital episode data and identifies the diagnoses, procedures, and other variables which determine allocation to an HRG.

HRGs have been developed in the UK as a result of dissatisfaction with the US-developed Diagnosis Related Groups (DRGs). They were developed initially within the context of the Resource Management Initiative. They were developed by the National Casemix Office, a body within the Information Management Group (IMG) of the NHS Executive. A programme to define HRGs was undertaken with 15 panels of specialty based clinical consultants who reconsidered the diagnoses and procedure codes pertinent to their work and clustered them into groups.

The HRG system has been adopted by the NHS Executive as the currency for future contract negotiations. Purchasers and providers are expected to use HRG costs either as the basis of contracts or as a factor in establishing overall contract prices.

HRGs are available to all purchasers and providers since they are based on information contained within the Contract Minimum Data Set which is collected for every inpatient and day case episode.

Total patient activity

Information on total patient activity levels can be obtained from the patient administration system. The PAS data can be manipulated to provide a wealth of information, but looking at the following information by year and for each specialty will provide a good starting point:

- number of new outpatient visits

- number of follow-up outpatient visits

- number of elective admissions

- number of emergency admissions

- average length of stay by specialty for each type of admission

- number of day cases and day cases as a percentage of all electives

- number of A&E visits.

This data should be compared over a three-year period in order to examine changes taking place within specialties. In the current climate the type of changes expected over a three-year period would be reductions in average length of stay, increases in day surgery, and possible decreases in the number of follow-up visits. Given national trends, there may also be an increase in emergency admissions.

Ward analysis

The next level of analysis is a ward analysis. This is something that is not routinely done and yet provides a great deal of valuable information. It can indicate periods when beds were closed, which consultants are the greatest users of which beds, which beds are under-utilized and which beds are over-utilized. This data should be available from the PAS system; it should be examined for at least two years and should include the following for each ward:

- the number of beds and their allocation by specialty/consultant

- the average numbers of beds available

- the total bed days used

- the average percentage occupancy

- the average length of stay by specialty/consultant

- the number of day cases by specialty/consultant

- the number of ward attenders by specialty/consultant
- the number of bed days used by each consultant

The information obtained from this analysis is described below.

The number of beds and the average number of beds available

This should be about the same. If the average number of beds available is considerably less than the number of beds, it indicates bed closures. The reasons for these closures should be reviewed; it may be a matter of refurbishment, shortage of staff, shortage of funds, a key consultant not being available, or simply too many beds.

The average percentage occupancy

The average percentage occupancy for the ward is a very clear indication of how effectively the beds are being used. Each hospital has its own interpretation of what an acceptable occupancy level should be and it will vary between specialties. In the case of specialties with a high emergency intake, for example, general medicine, occupancy rates can fluctuate substantially between different times of the year. Specialties which are primarily elective should be able to maintain more consistent rates and at a high level.

Bed assignments

In most hospitals, beds are still assigned to specialties or consultants. As changes have taken place in average lengths of stay and increases in day case procedures the necessary bed adjustments have often not taken place. Some examples of the most common type of poor bed utilization are described in Box 5.2.

Day cases

It is interesting to see the level of day case admissions to each ward. If the hospital has a dedicated day case unit there may be few ward day cases. In a situation with large numbers of ward day cases it may mean that there are some consultants who prefer to have their patients on their own ward, or that the day case unit has reached its full capacity and consultants are having to admit their day cases on to wards.

The number of ward attenders

Some specialties are renowned for their number of 'ward attenders', for example, paediatrics, endocrinology, ophthalmology. However, there is a need

---

Box 5.2: Examples of poor bed utilization

Urology

Beds assigned to urology are frequently either under-utilized or being used by other specialties or consultants, as a large number of common procedures are now done on a day case basis.

General medicine

Beds are frequently heavily utilized, especially during periods of heavy emergency admissions. The ward analysis will show the degree to which medical consultants are using beds on non-medical wards, i.e. borrowing beds from other specialties.

Paediatrics

Low utilization of paediatric beds is frequently seen; this can result from a combination of factors including: reductions in the average length of stay, a change in the age structure of the catchment area, seasonal fluctuations, or children being admitted on to other wards. Unlike in other specialties where excess beds may be borrowed by other specialties this does not usually occur in paediatrics. If the hospital does not follow the nationally recommended policy that all children should be treated on paediatric wards, it will be necessary to check the number of children admitted into non-paediatric beds, in order to accurately assess the need for paediatric beds.

---

to check on high volumes, namely, what are they there for; are they being recorded accurately as 'ward attenders'?

Bed days used by each consultant

There can be a wide variation in bed days used by consultants within the same specialty. This may be explained by case mix or differences in average length of stay or volume of patients treated. These differences are discussed in more detail under the next section on specialty analysis.

Where a trust has multiple hospital sites and may have beds from one specialty located in different hospitals, it is essential to compare use within specialties on the different sites.

Specialty analysis

From the foregoing analyses a picture will be emerging of the level of patient activity in the different specialties. The specialty analysis will examine each specialty in more detail and compare performance in terms of length of stay, rates of day surgery (if appropriate) with national data, and look for recent changes in modes of treatment or planned changes. It will also examine these factors on an individual consultant basis.

Average length of stay (ALOS)

ALOS is a major factor in the determination of future bed needs. Due to new modes of practice and surgical techniques ALOS has decreased dramatically in most specialties over recent years. As a first step the ALOS for each specialty should be compared with the ALOS for the specialty as available from sources such as the National Health Service indicators, regional data, or information from benchmarking groups. (The National Health Service indicators should be used with caution as the data is currently about two years out of date. Depending upon developments in the field, ALOS can be reduced significantly over a two-year period.)

If the ALOS is comparable to or below the national or other comparative level, then the specialty can be considered to have achieved an acceptable length of stay. If the ALOS is higher than the national average then it would appear that there are opportunities for improvement. At this point it would be useful to examine the ALOS by consultant within the specialty, as it may be that one or two consultants are raising the average with exceptionally long lengths of stay. There may be some good explanation for this in terms of case mix and the types of conditions those consultants are treating; if this is not the case, it could be a matter of consultants not changing old habits.

In some cases of longer than average lengths of stay, consultants may justify this by the age of their patients, claiming their patient base is older and therefore need longer stays. The National Health Service indicators for length of stay are also provided by age group, so comparisons of this nature are easy to make.

Although average lengths of stay in most specialties have been decreasing, the rate of decrease is already slowing down and there must come a point when further reductions will not occur; in some instances there could be increases. A reduction in hospitalization through improved admission procedures or an increase in day cases will mean that the patients admitted are those who are sicker or more dependent and will have longer lengths of stay.

Day cases

Another factor affecting future bed needs is the rate of days cases currently being undertaken and the rate projected for the future. This will primarily affect the following specialties: general surgery and urology, orthopaedics, ENT, ophthalmology, and gynaecology. The National Health Service indicators provide data by specialty on the national average and the maximum number of day cases as a percentage of elective admissions. By comparing these with the hospital's performance the level by which day cases can be expected to increase can be determined.

In July 1994 the NHS Executive's Performance Management Directorate urged purchasers to achieve a target of 60 per cent of all elective surgery performed as day cases by 1997–98. Some procedures such as abortion, D&C, myringotomy, cystoscopy, and excision of ganglions are being carried out on a day basis in 70–80 per cent of health authorities. But for procedures such as cataract removal, hernia repair, and varicose vein ligation the range is much wider. The range for cataracts is between 10 and 70 per cent.

The day case scenario is changing all the time; the introduction of the short-acting anaesthetic propofol (Diprivan) is making patients with asthma and other chronic illnesses eligible for day surgery where previously they would not have been considered. The drug is also making it possible to do longer operations on a day basis. As such developments occur and are implemented the targets for day surgery will change.

A study conducted in early 1996 by the London Health Economics Consortium[1] concluded that it was important not to overestimate the impact of increases in day case work on inpatient requirements, as in many cases the growth may represent new work, not substitution for existing inpatient work. An example of this was the growth in gastroendoscopy, an area where there was little previous inpatient work recorded. The study also found that where there was a fall in some inpatient procedures this was always less than the corresponding increase in day cases.

Differences between consultants

An analysis of the patient activity levels of consultants in the same specialty will often reveal large differences. Sometimes this can be explained by differences in case mix, but often it is a matter of individual practice patterns or certain consultants receiving higher levels of referrals than their colleagues. Managers need to be aware of these variations in planning future services, for example, if a very productive consultant is about to retire, how will this affect the volume of patients of the service?; or if a consultant who receives far more GP referrals than his colleagues is about to retire, can the same number of referrals be expected or will some go to competing hospitals?

It should also be noted that there is a considerable variation between districts in medical staffing levels, which is not accounted for by variations in workload. One study has revealed at least a three-fold variation in the workload of consultants, junior doctors, and nurses in 31 district general hospitals in three regions.

Specialty business plans

As part of this analysis it will be necessary to meet with the consultants in each specialty to determine where they see their service going in the future and what plans they may have to provide new services or increase/decrease existing services.

Bed census

In any inpatient facility the appropriate and efficient use of beds is very important. A bed census examines the appropriateness of care for all patients in the hospital at a given time. Such a census needs to be carried out by clinical staff and in the case of a large hospital can be expensive and time-consuming to conduct. Many of the censuses that have been conducted to date have been done in the smaller community hospitals. In any large acute unit it is a better use of resources to limit conducting a bed census to areas which have already been identified as having problems from the other review activities discussed in this chapter.

A bed census will identify both good and bad practice and will often lead to changes in hospital procedures or clinical practice. The type of problems identified include:

- poor admission polices, i.e. the patient should not have been admitted

- discharge delayed due to lack of suitable placement options

- discharge delayed due to lack of hospital resources, e.g. physiotherapy

- hospital stay longer than necessary due to delays in scheduling needed diagnostic tests, e.g. X-rays, endoscopies etc.

- consultant only does ward rounds on certain days, so no patients can be discharged on the days the consultant does not attend

- patient stays extended due to lack of patient transport or difficulties for relatives/friends to collect them on certain days.

Many of these problems can be resolved by better internal organization or changes in practice. An ongoing problem for many hospitals is the lack of an appropriate facility to discharge the patients to. The bed census can identify the extent of such problems and give the hospital more credibility in negotiating these difficulties with the community carers and the local authorities in question.

Bed censuses are not a new approach, but critical to their success is involving the consultants and nursing staff caring for the patient in the review. It cannot be just a paper exercise of reviewing the case notes after the patient is discharged. The notes need to be reviewed and then any questions concerning the appropriateness of care raised with the consultants and nurses for their explanation of why things were done in a certain way. Like any other tool, this type of analysis is useful only in so far as managers are prepared to use the results.

Audit Commission indicators for monitoring the use of beds

In 1992 the Audit Commission conducted a study on the use of medical beds in acute care hospitals (op. cit.). The study found large variations between districts, both in the availability of beds and in the efficiency with which beds were used. They found problems in five areas:

1   *Admissions*: some admissions were inappropriate.

2   *Placement*: Some patients are placed on inappropriate wards and subsequently moved.

3   *Length of stay*: many unexplained variations in lengths of stay and a lack of consensus between consultants on the most appropriate periods of stay.

4   *Discharge*: discharge procedures are poorly organized; frequent delays due to arranging transport, take home medicines, nursing home places, etc.

5   *Bed availability*: no adjustments to the number of beds available; 60 per cent of hospitals had not reviewed bed allocations to specialties for at least a year.

The Audit Commission recommended that managers and clinicians needed to establish their own set of operational indicators which are agreed to be accurate reflections of performance. They suggested a possible set of indicators for monitoring the use of hospital beds and they are shown in Box 5.3.

Box 5.3: Possible indicators for monitoring the use of hospital beds

Indicator	Provides an assessment of
Number of referrals per 1000 population for each GP	Extent of appropriate referrals
Time spent waiting in the A&E department before placement	Adequacy of the number of available beds
Number of patients placed on ward of another specialty	Adequacy of the number of beds for each specialty
Average number of ward transfers per patient	Compliance with transfer procedures
Length of stay profiles for selected common conditions and consultants	Consistency of clinical decisions
Discharge by day of the week by consultant, with ward rounds marked	Whether there are sufficient ward rounds or delegation of discharge decisions
Reasons for being in hospital for all patients on a particular day	What proportion of patients need to be in hospital
Proportion of patients with length of stay greater than some benchmark	Proper functioning of discharge procedures
Time of day patients leave hospital	Appropriateness of timing of discharge and ward rounds
Number of empty beds each ward has each day	Bed allocations
Reasons for refusal of admission and subsequent history	Effectiveness of admission screening arrangements

The Commission noted that correcting the inefficiencies in these areas would result in a reduced need for inpatient beds. As an example they estimated that if all districts reduced their lengths of stay to those of the lowest 25 per cent (after allowing for the effect of age), and matched bed numbers more closely to their use, the current (1992) level of medical inpatient treatment in England could be provided with 27 000 beds or almost one-third fewer beds.

As part of their recommendations to this study the Audit Commission suggested that hospitals consider the costs and benefits of introducing different types of beds, including:

- observation beds

- admission wards

- five-day medical wards

- planned investigation units

- patient hotels.

Review of competition

It is essential to understand who are the main competitors and what are their strengths and weaknesses. In some cases the main competitors will be different for different specialties.

In the large city situation like London it is often very difficult to know instinctively who the real competition is to each service. The consultants are likely to have the best idea on this issue. An analysis of referring GP practice by specialty will give some indication of from where the patients are coming. If the patients are coming from different areas then there is clearly no geographic basis for competition and that particular service must either be well known and respected or the only one in the area. If in another specialty the patients tend to be coming from the same area, probably in close proximity to the hospital, it can be assumed that many referrals are going elsewhere and it is necessary to know to which hospitals they are going.

In some smaller towns or rural areas the competition may be much less intense, probably only affecting the patients living on the borders of the hospital catchment area who may be equidistant from another hospital. In this case it is necessary to know the numbers of patients involved and the potential impact of gaining or losing such patients.

Every hospital needs to compile information about all the provider units in the surrounding area (both NHS and private), from whom purchasers may obtain competing services. The type of information that is likely to be useful includes:

- profiles of the health care services that they provide

- variation in the level and quality of services provided

Box 5.4: Analysis of current patient activity and utilization of resources: types of analysis and information required

Contracts
- major purchasers
- level of service by specialty
- purchaser plans

Total patient activity
- no. of new outpatient visits
- no. of follow-up outpatient visits
- no. of elective admissions
- no. of emergency admissions
- ALOS by admission type
- no. of A&E visits
- no. of day cases

Bed census
- examines the appropriate use of beds on a per patient basis

Ward analysis
- assigned no. of beds
- no. of beds available
- no. of bed days used
- average occupancy
- ALOS
- no. of pt. days by cons.
- ALOS by consultant
- no. of day cases by cons.
- no. of ward attenders by cons.
- bed swaps between specialties

Specialty analysis
- admissions/spec.
- bed days/spec.
- admissions/cons.
- bed days/cons.
- ALOS/spec.
- ALOS/cons.
- new out-pt./spec.
- new out-pt./cons.
- f-up out-pt./spec.
- f-up out-pt/cons.
- specialty plans

Review competition
- services offered
- strengths and weaknesses
- plans for change in capacity

Summary of patient activity and bed use
- consolidates findings from the reviews
- identifies areas of under/over-utilization
- identifies planned changes in modes of care/levels of activity
- identifies poor practices

- travel times from the centres of population served

- overlaps with the population served by the hospital

- recent and planned developments to increase capacity or quality, or to reduce costs

- known constraints, for example on capacity or accessibility.

As well as individual competitor analysis, competitive reviews should include an assessment of the pattern of service provision in the locality, its deficiencies and potential for improvement, both in current and future terms.

Summary of patient activity

Once the analysis is complete the findings should be compiled into a summary report on all patient activity and more detailed reports on each individual specialty. The process is summarized in the form of a flow chart in Box 5.4.

Reference

1   Edwards N. (1966) Day for night. *Health Service Journal.* **106** (5502).

6

Projecting bed needs

Introduction

At the present stage in the evolution of health care the significance of the bed as the unit by which the adequate provision of acute hospital services can be measured is declining. Despite this recognition that they are not always the most appropriate unit of measure, inpatient beds are still used as the indicator of the quantity and quality of health service provision. Health service planners have long sought more appropriate measures for the provision of services, but the complexities of quantifying health services in terms of outputs and outcomes has retained the focus on beds.

In this environment of rapid changes in medical science and technology, it is difficult to project bed needs with any accuracy for longer than five years or at the most 10 years, yet most capital plans require much longer projections. This chapter will examine methodologies for projecting bed needs and the range of factors which need to be taken into consideration.

In previous chapters the need for managers to have vision and to think strategically in order to place their organization and its services in the most appropriate position for the future has been emphasized. In support of such strategies it is essential to know how the current provision of beds relates to current need and to project future bed needs under different scenarios. From this starting point any vision of service mix and volume for the future can be translated into beds and other facilities required.

Building a hospitalization model

The simplest way to project hospital bed needs is to construct a very basic, relational database computer model. The computer model will then permit different scenarios to be created and tested and allow a range of bed needs to be projected based upon different events taking place. The structure of the model and its operation will depend upon the software used and is therefore not discussed in detail in this context.

In Chapters 4 and 5 the importance of understanding the catchment population and analysing current patient activity was discussed. The information from these activities provides the basic data required for building a hospitalization model and projecting bed needs. To build the model the following data sets are required.

The population of the catchment area

This should be OPCS data for the current year and projections for five and 10 years, divided by sex and into the following age groups:

- 0–4 years
- 5–14
- 15–24
- 25–44
- 45–64
- 65–74
- 75–84
- 85 +

The age groups as presented above are in standard use in health service planning as the divisions chosen can be easily related to the variations in levels of service utilization which occur with age and sex differences.

The number of finished consultant episodes/admissions by specialty for the most recent year

As the use of FCEs as a unit of measure becomes less popular the number of admissions can be used and is actually preferable as it provides more definitive and accurate information. This data needs to be broken down by age group and sex and divided by type of admission, namely: elective, emergency, day case.

Average length of stay (ALOS)

This should also be broken down into specialties, age groups, sex, and types of admission.

Hospitalization rate

Using the population data and the number of FCEs or admissions a hospitalization rate can be calculated by specialty and age.

$$\text{Hospitalization rate} = \frac{\text{total admissions/FCEs by age and specialty}}{\text{number of district residents in the age band}}$$

This is always expressed as a rate per 1000 population.

Bed days required

Bed days required are calculated by multiplying the number of FCEs for each specialty and age group by the average length of stay for that specialty and age group.

Beds needed

Once the total number of bed days required has been calculated for each specialty, the number of beds required will be determined by the occupancy level. An example of this is provided in Box 6.1.

Comparison of beds required with beds available

It is essential in projecting bed needs that the adequacy and effective utilization of current beds in each specialty is assessed as a first step. Just because a

---

Box 6.1: Beds required at different occupancy levels

At a 90 per cent occupancy level each bed will be occupied 329 days of the year, i.e. 365 days × 90/100
At 80 per cent occupancy level each bed will be occupied 292 days of the year
At 70 per cent occupancy level each bed will be occupied 256 days of the year

Example
If the total bed days required for a particular specialty are 165 000
The number of beds required at 90 per cent occupancy will be 502
The number of beds required at 80 per cent occupancy will be 565
The number of beds required at 70 per cent occupancy will be 645

The occupancy level makes a major difference to the numbers of beds required. In the above example the difference between operating at 70 per cent and 90 per cent is 143 beds, which is equivalent to five large wards.

certain number of beds are in operation, and have been the same for some time, it cannot be assumed that this is the correct number of beds for the level of service being delivered.

Once the number of beds required for each specialty, at different occupancy levels and lengths of stay consistent with best practice (as discussed in Chapter 4), has been calculated, a comparison of the number of beds currently required with the current beds available will indicate the degree to which the hospital is under- or over-bedded in each specialty, assuming that hospitalization rates remain the same. This is a very important starting point, as frequently in bed projections there are significant differences in some specialties between current beds available and projected beds. This difference, either up or down, can seem unrealistic, especially over a short period such as five years. However, the difference is often large because the current bed numbers are not appropriate for the level of service provided and projections have been made on the basis of 'best practice'. Starting with the knowledge of what the current bed level should be, as opposed to what it actually is, makes the projections seem much more realistic.

It should be noted that occupancy levels will differ between specialties. There is a justifiable case for using a lower occupancy level in specialties such as general medicine where the majority of admissions are emergencies and therefore not within the total control of bed management. In specialties such as general surgery, where the majority of admissions are elective, a higher level of occupancy could be utilized. However, even in specialties which are primarily elective, contingencies frequently arise and it is not realistic to calculate levels at higher than 85 per cent. The occupancy level for obstetric beds is usually calculated at 70–75 per cent and ITU or SCBU beds are calculated at 65–70 per cent.

Projecting bed needs

To calculate bed needs the future number of FCEs/admissions must be projected using the OPCS population projections. Table 6.1 shows a straight line extrapolation of FCEs by age group based upon the percentage increases or decreases in the population of the catchment area for the years 2000 and 2005. Once the projections are prepared it is essential to refine them by considering the eight factors discussed below.

1   Hospitalization rates

In Table 6.1 the extrapolated FCEs are based upon the assumption that current rates of hospitalization remain the same. This may not be an accurate assumption as hospitalization rates do change over time and there is a wide variation between different places in the UK and between the UK and other developed countries.

Table 6.1:   Gynaecology: projected FCEs for the year 2000 and 2005

| Year | FCEs by age groups | | | | | | | Total |
	0–14	15–24	25–44	45–64	65–74	75–84	85+	
1995–96	24	1700	3600	941	181	82	18	6546
Projected percentage change in the female population of catchment area								
2000	−0.81	−0.89	0.48	6.44	−3.49	6.23	14.92	
2005	−6.42	8.71	−3.39	14.51	−1.99	11.67	19.20	
Projected FCEs based on 1994–95 FCEs								
2000	24	1685	3617	1002	175	87	21	6611
2005	22	1848	3478	1078	177	92	22	6717

To understand how current hospitalization rates for the catchment population compare with those of other areas, data from the National Health Service indicators can be used. The indicators provide standardized hospitalization rates by age, sex, and specialty on both a health authority and a national basis. In instances where the trust rates are considerably higher or lower than the rates they are compared to, adjustments can be made to the projections.

In 1992–93, the hospitalization rate for acute specialties for England was 160 per 1000 population. The variation is illustrated by a rate of 129 per 1000 in Wolverhampton and 221 per 1000 in Manchester. Leeds had a rate of 195 per 1000, and as part of a review of acute hospital services in Leeds in 1995 a more detailed study was conducted in this area. This high pattern of demand was not found in all age groups. Children and young adults in Leeds used fewer beds per 1000 population than the national rate. However, middle-aged and older people used significantly more beds than would be expected. The study did not address the reasons for the high level of demand. There are many potential causes including historical patterns of care, inadequate provision of primary care services, poor home environment, and availability of beds, but in such cases further work needs to be done to understand the causes so that if they can be rectified appropriate adjustments can be made to the hospitalization rate used in the projection of bed needs.

2   Average length of stay

The impact of the average length of stay on the number of beds required was discussed in Chapter 5. It is suggested that average length of stay by specialty and age group be compared with the National Health Service indicators or other source such as a benchmarking group. In specialties where the trust's average length of stay is higher than those to which it is compared, bed requirements should be calculated on achieving improvements in this area.

3 Day cases

The impact of day cases was also discussed in Chapter 5. The bed needs should be projected with day case rates at the proposed national or regional targets.

4 Peaks and troughs of patient activity

Projections of bed needs over a period of a year as described above do not take into account the peaks and troughs of activity which occur in some specialties. In order to understand such swings of activity it is necessary to take two or three years' data and examine the number of FCEs and bed days used each month for each specialty. The specialties most affected by peaks and troughs of activity are those with a high rate of emergency admissions such as general medicine and paediatrics. In specialties with a high rate of elective admissions such as general surgery, there is some room for flexibility in periods of high emergency admissions, but usually only by cancelling elective admissions at short notice. This is a practice which should only be used as a last resort as it is very distressing for patients and their families and also discouraged by the Patient's Charter.

5 Waiting lists

As previously discussed, the Patient's Charter has set targets for waiting times for both new outpatient appointments and elective admissions. Whatever the current performance of the hospital with regard to waiting lists, future bed requirements should be projected on the assumption that waiting list targets as established by the Patient's Charter or purchaser will be achieved. This could mean increasing projected bed numbers, but only if the intent is there to provide the other support services needed, for example, theatre time.

6 The Patient's Charter

The main impact of the Patient's Charter on future bed requirements will be through meeting waiting time targets as discussed above. Other aspects, such as the right of patients to be treated on single sex wards and the needs of children in hospital, will have to be taken into account.

7 The *Health of the nation*

The *Health of the nation* strategy was discussed in Chapter 1 and it was noted that meeting the set targets is identified as a main objective for the NHS in the Secretary of State's Annual Priorities and Planning Guidance. Meeting targets may involve increasing hospital services and beds in areas of the country where the mortality and/or morbidity rates for the specified diseases are too high. Purchasers should be taking the lead in ensuring that adequate services are available in these areas.

8   Readmission rates

In view of the pressures to decrease average lengths of stay, hospitals should closely monitor readmission rates by procedure as part of the clinical audit process. If high readmission rates do occur and can be related to discharging patients prematurely then length of stay rates will have to be increased in the projection calculations.

Scenario planning

Medicial science and technology are changing so rapidly that it is difficult to project bed needs based upon present modes of medical practice. One way to handle this problem is to project a range of bed needs based on different scenarios. Such scenarios can take into account changes in practice patterns across a range of parameters and 'improvements' in efficiency and performance in certain areas. In the final analysis 'ranges' of bed numbers are not accurate enough for planning specific capital projects or looking at a large scale rationalization of services between sites, but they are useful for looking at the impact of different situations. The following are examples of often used scenarios:

- What would be the impact on the bed requirements for each specialty if all day cases were treated in a separate day case unit?

- What would be the impact on bed requirements for each specialty if all children (0–12 years) were treated on paediatric wards?

- What would be the impact on bed requirements for each specialty if an adolescent unit was established for all 13–16-year-olds?

- What would be the impact on day case and inpatient bed requirements if the purchasers stopped funding certain procedures, for example, wisdom teeth removal, myringotomy, D&C?

- What would be the impact on inpatient bed requirements of a patient hotel?

These are examples of what can be done very quickly using a computerized hospitalization model. The impact of such scenarios can be looked at both individually and cumulatively. It is the cumulative effect of what appears to be minor changes which can be useful to observe. Exercises of this nature provide a good indication of the impact on bed needs of different situations or courses of action which without such detailed calculation would be difficult to visualize accurately.

Other major factors to consider

Patient access

Access to medical care at any level is a combination of being able to get appointments and beds within a reasonable time and also physical access in terms of travel time and availability of transport. For the acute care sector the Patient's Charter has provided guidelines for access in terms of waiting times for new outpatient appointments and admissions for elective surgery. There are also national standards for response times to accident and emergency calls. All these factors have to be taken into consideration when making bed projections or planning to rationalize services between different sites.

Decisions to rationalize beds and/or outpatient services between sites need to take into consideration a number of physical factors including:

- reviewing where the patients will be coming from and how they will get to the proposed sites

- what percentage of the households have cars; will this be a major mode of transport?

- what are the current public transport services; are they adequate; will they need to be changed?

- how much time can patients and their families be expected to spend travelling to hospital services; what travelling time is considered reasonable by purchasers?

- access to services for groups of patients with specific problems must be examined, for example, the elderly, mothers with young children, the disabled. For these type of patients is there any scope to improve access by moving outpatient services into the community?

- can more diagnostic work be carried out in health centres or GP surgeries in order to reduce patient trips to hospital?

- can diagnostic testing be better organized in order that patients can receive a range of tests in just one visit; can testing be carried out at the time of the patient's first visit?

There has been a recent trend to develop outreach clinics in GP surgeries; on evaluation this has not always been successful. While it may offer the advantages to patients of seeing a consultant closer to home, in familiar surroundings, and can reduce waiting time, there can be serious disadvantages including ineffective use of consultant time, a need to eventually visit the hospital for tests which cannot be carried out in GP surgeries, and increased administration for both the GP surgery and the trust.

With forward planning and some vision and imagination there is much that can be done to improve patient access to acute care services above present levels even while reducing the number of beds and hospital sites available.

Medical staffing

The impact of reducing junior doctors' hours has already been discussed in terms that it will lead to an increase in the more senior ranks and more consultant-led care. The impact of this on bed needs will require some consideration. In some specialties the availability of more consultants could increase the number of referrals and therefore the need for beds and other services. In other specialties the availability of more experienced senior medical staff may actually reduce emergency admissions and lead to earlier discharges. This type of impact will need to be considered on a specialty by specialty basis. In a similar way department plans to offer new services or increase the number of consultants to cope with demand must be taken into consideration.

Theatre utilization

Studies have shown that there is a wide variation in theatre utilization between acute care hospitals around the country. Any review and projection of bed needs must include a review of theatre utilization, as any changes in bed numbers, medical staffing, and modes of medical practice must be supported by an adequate provision of operating theatres.

In many hospitals allocation of theatre time is still done on a historical basis and may remain largely unchanged despite unused capacity, wide variations in use by individual specialties and clinicians, and repeated cancellation of particular sessions. Before any decisions are taken on the number and type of theatres available, a thorough review of the current situation should be accomplished. Such a review should be conducted on a specialty and individual clinician basis and examine:

- the number of sessions allocated to each consultant

- the number of cancelled sessions and the reasons

- the number of cases performed in terms of emergency, elective, and day case

- the length of sessions

- the percentage of time each theatre is not utilized excluding planned maintenance and time set aside for emergency admissions.

Projecting future theatre requirements must take into account:

- current utilization and improvements which can be achieved

- future levels of service and modes of practice, for example, keyhole surgery requires more theatre time than conventional surgery; the impact of increased levels of day surgery, and whether this will be done in the regular theatres or in a special day surgery unit

- can theatre utilization be improved by better bed management, for example, are theatre sessions being cancelled because beds are unavailable for elective admissions?

Determining beds by the number of patient episodes

The inquiry into London hospitals led by Professor Sir Bernard Tomlinson recommended that acute care hospitals have between 10 and 14 beds per 1000 FCEs by 1998. This target was originally based on cross-sectional performance analysis carried out by North West Thames RHA. In a study published in January 1995, Mallender Hancock Associates tried to assess how far London acute trusts are from achieving the suggested targets and how applicable the measure is as a general performance target for London hospitals.[1]

The study concluded that most hospitals were operating within the benchmarks suggested by the Tomlinson inquiry, on average at 12.4 beds per 1000 FCEs for acute care specialties. There were differences in the performance of individual hospitals which may be attributable to differences in the profile of the hospital with regard to the proportion of activity which is:

- provided on an emergency basis

- provided to elderly patients

- provided within those specialties with higher than average lengths of stay, for example, general medicine, trauma, and orthopaedics.

While benchmarking the number of beds per 1000 FCEs can be a useful management tool, it must be used with extreme caution. Given that there are major differences between acute care hospitals in terms of specialty mix, case mix, and patient characteristics, such 'rules of thumb' cannot substitute for more detailed and scientific projections.

Summary

A summary of the process for projecting bed needs is shown in Box 6.2.

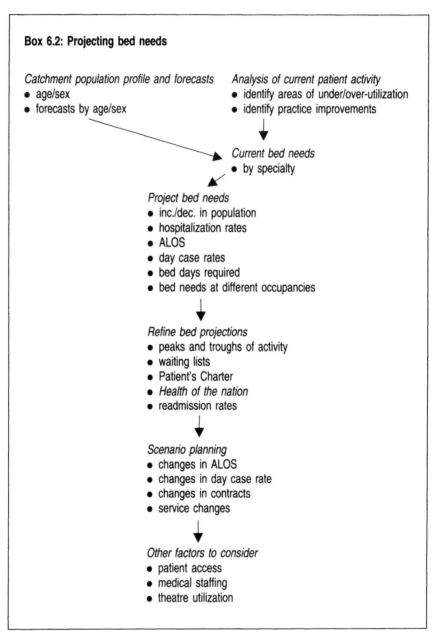

Box 6.2: Projecting bed needs

Catchment population profile and forecasts
- age/sex
- forecasts by age/sex

Analysis of current patient activity
- identify areas of under/over-utilization
- identify practice improvements

Current bed needs
- by specialty

Project bed needs
- inc./dec. in population
- hospitalization rates
- ALOS
- day case rates
- bed days required
- bed needs at different occupancies

Refine bed projections
- peaks and troughs of activity
- waiting lists
- Patient's Charter
- *Health of the nation*
- readmission rates

Scenario planning
- changes in ALOS
- changes in day case rate
- changes in contracts
- service changes

Other factors to consider
- patient access
- medical staffing
- theatre utilization

Reference

1   Mallender J. (1995) *Comparing throughput in London hospitals*. Mallender Hancock Associates.

7

Site and facilities appraisal

Introduction

Any process of rationalization of services will usually result in capital expenditures for either renovations or new buildings and such costs will be an important element in the decision to rationalize services. This chapter briefly describes some of the major estates' issues which must be considered when making the decision to change, move, or resite services.

Once a clear vision of future services and levels of service has been developed, consideration must be given to the facilities needed to deliver such services. For all trusts this will entail reviewing current facilities and developing a series of options for the future, together with the costs associated with each option. There will be very few trusts with the opportunity of a totally new build on a green field site; for most organizations it will be a matter of trying to achieve the best fit between the existing estate and future service needs.

Single versus multiple sites

Many acute care trusts in the UK provide services from more than one site, so the decision to close beds or rationalize services in other ways often involves the closing of one or more sites. This not only reduces the estates' operating costs but can also result in less duplication of services and equipment and reduced management and administrative costs. This situation is in contrast to the one currently being faced by many acute care hospitals in the United States, where operation from single sites is the norm and as the number of acute care beds is reduced, hospitals are left with a lot of space for which they are having difficulty finding cost-effective uses.

For single site trusts in the UK, reducing the number of beds often frees up space that is badly needed for other services or functions. Many inner-city single site trusts have almost insurmountable problems of old and inappropriate buildings, with no room for expansion and inadequate access and parking. For them the key decision is what capital changes need to be made to continue operating from the present site or the feasibility of building on a new site.

Delivering acute care from multiple sites, while sometimes necessary, can negate against ever being able to achieve the high levels of operational efficiency expected from today's hospitals. Having inpatient beds on multiple sites limits flexibility in terms of specialty mix. Some specialties need to be together, for example, obstetrics and gynaecology because they use the same consultants. Other specialties would benefit from being in close proximity, for example, gynaecology and medical oncology, or obstetrics and paediatrics. Clinical support services such as theatres and therapies often have to be duplicated on all the sites.

All or some sites will be experiencing the problems associated with older buildings such as high energy and maintenance costs. Having one site with these problems is expensive, but having to operate several sites all with similar problems can have a major impact on the costs of patient care.

In the process of the rationalization of services between sites there is often one site which is the obvious choice for making the primary site. It may be larger and/or newer than other sites, has space to expand, has good access by road and has ample car parking, or other factors which makes it the natural choice for concentrating the services. In other instances there will be several sites with no obvious primary site and there may be serious problems of patient access to be addressed in terms of moving services from one site to another. In the case of a single site, reducing bed numbers can be an opportunity to reassess overall site use. In either event a detailed review of the sites is essential and this chapter outlines some of the key components of such a review, together with addressing the topical issue of patient focused care and how this can be built into plans as services are relocated.

Estates' functional content and space utilization

As a starting point it is essential to have an inventory of what all the space on the site or different sites is used for and how much space each of the services is occupying. In most organizations an up to date, detailed, functional content analysis does not exist. The preparation of this, whether done in-house or using outside consultants, will be expensive. However, it is the first step in an exercise of this nature and will provide a lot of valuable information.

The functional content and space utilization analysis usually comprises two components, a walk through the facilities and meetings with all the departments concerned.

The 'walk through'

This is generally conducted by 'walking through' all the buildings and noting on detailed floor plans what each room or other space is used for, and also to update any structural changes which have taken place to the detailed floor plans being used.

Meetings with department heads

Meetings should be held with each head of department or section to discuss the adequacy of their present space and their anticipated future requirements. This part of the analysis is also a good communications and public relations exercise as it provides a forum for departments to make their needs known and to feel that they have been consulted before any final decisions are reached.

It should be emphasized that the outcome of such an analysis should not take the format of a 'shopping list' for the ideal space requirements. As medical technology and modes of care are changing so rapidly the amount and type of space required by a department can change significantly even in a short time. A good example of this phenomenon is clinical imaging where, with new developments, space needs have changed dramatically. Overnight beds are now often required by this service for carrying out both diagnostic and treatment procedures, and the proliferation of new equipment means that the department is often scattered around the hospital or split between sites. The rationalization of services presents the opportunity to remedy this and many similar situations, which can result in better staff morale and more efficient working procedures.

Following the functional content analysis a space utilization report should be prepared using the data and information obtained. The space utilization report should describe the following areas:

- the location of facilities on the site (sites)

- the current patient accommodation

- the advantages and disadvantages of the present site layouts

- the volume of building space per inpatient bed

- the amount of space which is unused or underutilized in the buildings

- the amount of land which is unused or underutilized on the site

- the volume of space utilized by each department

- the current and future space needs of each department.

This report will form the basis for developing the options for service and site rationalization.

Site constraints

The sites should all be reviewed for constraints which may be a barrier to further developments or to selling unwanted sites. Such constraints would include planning issues, listed buildings, conservation area restrictions, or inadequate vehicular access to the sites. In some instances sites may be bounded by drainage systems or power lines which represent a limit to permitted development.

In an article in the *Nursing Standard* in January 1995, Charles Ward claimed that estates of over 45 000 acres make the NHS one of the country's largest landowners and that almost half of this land is now surplus to requirements. With the size and number involved, finding new uses and buyers for redundant hospitals can be difficult, particularly in a depressed property market. Sites are often in environmentally sensitive areas or have buildings of architectural or historic interest. Some of the most common constraints are described below.

Green belt

The Department of the Environment has formulated special planning policies for when buildings are in a green belt and has listed the following range of options in order of preference:

- reuse for purposes which would normally be acceptable in a green belt, e.g. agriculture, forestry, outdoor sport, cemeteries, institutions within extensive grounds

- if reuse within conventional green belt policies is not viable, then conversions of the building to other uses may be considered

- if the site has to be redeveloped because the buildings cannot be converted then the impact on the green belt should be no greater than the original hospital use

- when reuse of buildings is not an option they may be demolished immediately, rather than being left to rot.

Poorly documented titles

Poorly documented titles can also affect prospects for reusing or redeveloping redundant hospitals. Many buildings date from the nineteenth century and came under the Department of Health in 1948 when the NHS was established. Titles are often old, unregistered, piecemeal, and incomplete; such title defects often only come to light when the building is about to be sold.

Deed restrictions

As many of the old hospital buildings were donated there are often deed restrictions, the most common limiting the use of the land to that of a hospital. In other instances, the land may be leasehold with tight restrictions.

Listed buildings

The NHS owns about 820 buildings listed by the Department of National Heritage as being of architectural or historic interest. This is more than any other government body except for the Ministry of Defence. Many of these buildings are difficult to upgrade to accommodate modern health care, and such listing can frighten away potential buyers because of the planning restrictions and preservation orders that are associated with them.

Listing brings with it the obligation to prevent the building's physical deterioration. NHS Estates together with English Heritage have recently issued guidance on dealing with listed buildings. The first step recommended by the guide is to hire expert advice. The NHS Estates and English Heritage have set up a taskforce to review the entire list of historic buildings in the health service and ensure a consistent standard of listing across the board.

A problem for managers trying to dispose of buildings is 'spot-listing'. Often spot-listing is used by pressure groups or local activists to block proposed closure of old hospitals. As long as a building is listed or under investigation for spot-listing, no physical alterations can be made without listed building consent. In rationalization spot-listing often occurs late in the process when the plans are being implemented. A trust could be relying on substantial revenue from the sale of a building to offset other necessary capital expenditures; spot-listing can substantially reduce the saleable value of such buildings.

The surroundings of the sites must be considered in terms of location; for example, in a strictly residential area, semi-industrial area, or inner-city area restrictions on site rationalization or further developments may be imposed. The expansion of services in a residential area is often very difficult unless adequate parking facilities and public transport access can also be provided.

If further building on a site is being considered as one of the options available, a topological survey will be required to ensure that building is possible and to identify any additional building costs which could arise from topological conditions.

Condition appraisal

Central to developing the options for rationalization is the condition of the existing buildings and the associated costs of any backlog maintenance. Monitoring the physical condition of all buildings is an ongoing responsibility of the estates department. For the purpose of this type of exercise the condition of buildings needs to be rated on some form of scale. A four-point scale of high standard, acceptable standard, below standard, and unacceptable is sufficient for this purpose. This is usually presented as the percentage of space in each category for each site.

The condition appraisal should include both building and engineering conditions. In recent years many hospitals have 'face-lifted' areas for good front of house presentation, while ignoring the maintenance of primary services. Detailed information on deferred and planned maintenance and estimated costs needs to be available as this will have an impact on the cost of the different options under consideration.

Site services appraisal

A detailed assessment will need to be made of the services at each site, in terms of their age, condition, current adequacy of service, and future requirements if services are expanded. This would include:

• the primary energy source for heating and hot water

• the mains cold water supplies for both potable drinking water and fire fighting supplies

• a *legionella* survey and report

• details of the medical gases infrastructure and condition

• fire alarm system

• telephone and data links

• electrical system.

Having examined the energy services infrastructure it would be desirable to undertake a complete energy audit of the sites to examine the efficiency with which the individual departments and buildings utilize the energy supplied to them. The energy performance of each area should be assessed in terms of an overview of the efficiency of building fabric and the design and control of mechanical and electrical services. Such an audit should culminate in identifying the scope for energy saving measures and the cost of such measures.

Statutory requirements

This category covers a wide range of conditions which may represent a risk to staff, patients, or building fabric. The range of matters taken into consideration should include the following:

- extent of fire precaution measures

- presence of asbestos

- environmental health issues

- level of deterioration of fabric or service giving cause for concern

- changes in legislation standards.

The effects arising from the loss of Crown immunity with trust status and ongoing changes and upgrading of legislative standards can mean major capital expenditures are required to bring older buildings into compliance. The costs associated with meeting statutory requirements can make a major difference when the costs of the proposed options are under consideration. For example, it has been estimated that large hospitals built in the 1960s and 1970s could face bills of over £2 million to remove all the asbestos on their premises.

Location and accessibility

When planning to rationalize services between sites the location and accessibility of sites are of major concern. The key questions which must be answered in this regard are:

- where is the building located in relation to the population to be served?

- what are the major roads providing access?

- what is the public transport provided to the site?

- are any major changes planned in roads and traffic patterns?

- what are the car parking facilities at the site?

An estimate of the number of visitors to the site on a daily basis can be made from the number of outpatient visits each day and the number of inpatients and potential visitors to patients. Estimates should also be made of the number of visitors who travel by car and those who come by public transport. The number of staff working at the site and the means by which they travel to work is also a key factor.

In changing the site of services, transportation, car parking, and access by road will be of key concern in any public consultation process. This will be of concern not only to the patients and their visitors, but also to residents living in close proximity to the site and to the effect any increase in traffic will have on their daily lives. Before taking any plans to public consultation it is essential that access is addressed in detail and solutions are put forward in terms of increased parking and increased public transportation services. By reviewing the information on how many patients are coming from each area it should be possible to determine travel times by both private and public transport and put forward solutions for those who will have poor access by public transport.

The impact on staff should also be thoroughly investigated. The impact on low paid staff in a move from one site to another can be particularly hard in terms of increased transportation costs and travel time. In areas of high employment it could mean staff leaving for jobs closer to home and may impact on the hospital's ability to deliver services. In some instances it may be necessary to organize specific staff transport.

Patient focused care

The rationalization of services and the incumbent changes to buildings or sites provides an opportunity to restructure facilities to better meet the needs of patient care. The concept of patient focused care (PFC) is one means of achieving this.

The term 'patient focused care' embraces a variety of concepts in health care provision. The underlying principle is to improve the patient's experience. It represents a re-examination of the way care is delivered in a hospital (or other settings) and a realignment of care delivery so that the patient is at the centre.

The concept began in the USA as a result of the work of management consultants. The consultants, who had been analysing and improving manufacturing processes in the car industry, applied what they had learned to a sample of acute care hospitals. They concluded that the hospital was a very fragmented organization and that the fragmentation worked to the detriment of patient care. They claimed that the professional groups had developed unassailable barriers, buildings and processes were designed around outdated concepts, there was extensive staff specialization, and direct care staff were spending up to 60 per cent of their time on paperwork and transport arrangements.

There is no single model of PFC. The models being pursued in the USA and UK place different emphases on different components, but the three basic elements are:

1   restructuring of services and physical regrouping of facilities

2   restructuring teams of staff caring for patients and redesigning jobs with associated multi-skilling

3   the development of care protocols for clinical conditions.

PFC attempts to restructure the organization of care according to three principles:

1   group things together physically; avoid cross-scheduling to another department

2   cross-train staff to mix tasks from different professions and return tasks to teams close to the patient

3   introduce clinical protocols to pre-plan the sequence of events during specific incidents of care.

From the perspective of this chapter it is the physical aspects of patient focused care which are being highlighted as worth consideration when analysing existing sites. In an article in *Hospital Development* in May 1993, Draper and Shani[1] describe the physical structuring of a patient focused hospital. Such a facility would comprise:

- *an acute care centre* with five or six operational units in place of 18–20 wards. Each operational unit would be like a mini hospital with its own operating theatres, intensive care, radiology, ultrasound, laboratory, pharmacy, administration, and support facilities. Patients would be admitted, treated, and discharged from within the unit. The number of beds in each operational unit will depend upon the planned workload of the unit and its function. The authors indicate that for adult general surgery the optimum size of the unit would be 100–130 beds, supported by two or three operating theatres, an endoscopy room, one X-ray room, a laboratory unit, and ultrasound facilities.

- *a day care diagnostic centre* which will have outpatient clinics, rehabilitation, and day surgery. Each outpatient clinic will have multi-function rooms for examination, dressings, ECG, blood and urine tests, etc. Each clinic, where appropriate, will have routine X-ray and laboratory facilities. Rehabilitation will be closely associated with outpatient clinics. Day surgery will be a separate unit with its own beds, operating theatres, laboratories, and other facilities.

- *a diagnostics unit*; about 15–20 per cent of diagnostic procedures require expensive equipment and highly skilled staff. The CT scanner, MRI, radio-isotope scanning, and other pathology services will be grouped together centrally. This diagnostic unit will act as a referral unit for all the hospital units and for GP services.

- *support services*; institutional management, computing, laundry, pharmacy, catering, and stores will remain centralized, but will be much smaller as each operational unit will have its own administration facilities, stores for sterile supplies, linen, housekeeping, pharmaceutical goods, and cook–chill regeneration pantry.

The authors claim that a patient focused hospital will require about 15 per cent less floor space than a conventional hospital. The decentralization associated with PFC may increase equipment costs by almost 40 per cent, but the total capital cost is still estimated to be 10–11 per cent less than in a conventional hospital.

In the context of this text, a case is not being made either for or against patient focused care. A new building or major renovations do present the opportunity to restructure the traditional ways of delivering services and all alternatives warrant serious consideration at this stage.

Future implications for acute care health facilities

Acute care hospitals have experienced many changes in design and trends since their original inception. The Nightingale wards, which in their day were a major innovation in hospital design and are still widespread in older UK hospitals, are being replaced by smaller groupings of beds with centralized nursing stations. The future design of acute care facilities will no doubt be different yet again, but the following factors will play a role:

- *fewer hospital beds*: substitution of ambulatory care, community care, and day cases will reduce bed needs

- *fewer hospitals*: closure and consolidation is likely as trusts merge and rationalize their services on to fewer sites

- *replacement facilities*: hospitals of the future will be smaller with substantially fewer acute inpatient beds: around 200–300 beds for community hospitals and 400–500 for regional tertiary facilities. Because the cost of modernization runs close to the cost of new construction, it may be more cost effective to build new downsized facilities

- *capital investment*: NHS and private capital funders will be more sceptical of large facility projects and will selectively invest capital in fewer hospitals which are smaller in size and accommodate ambulatory care

- *service/facility organization*: layout and design of future hospital facilities will be organized around patient flow, not beds, using management engineering studies and 'patient centred' care approaches

- *square footage*: future facilities will be built with more square feet per bed, to provide adequate space for ambulatory surgery and diagnostic equipment, and to provide greater flexibility in use

- *equipment*: the cost of equipping future facilities will increase, especially in the area of information technology; leasing is likely to be an increasingly popular alternative to purchasing, to avoid rapid obsolescence

- *patient expectations*: patient expectations for hospital facilities are changing and better and more pleasant surroundings are being demanded. It could be compared to the annual holiday business, where the seaside boarding houses which have survived are the ones which were quick to provide en suite rooms with TVs and telephones. To some degree NHS hospitals are still trading on the fact that they are 'free' at the point of contact so many patients will still accept gratefully whatever is doled out; but the days for this are numbered. This can already be seen in some areas; namely the ones where patients are well enough to make a choice between hospitals, as in maternity care.

Consideration of options

Once the site and facilities appraisal is complete the trust is in a position to identify a set of options available for achieving the planned rationalization of services. The process of options analysis is described in the next chapter.

Reference

1   Draper N, Shani S. (1993) Breaking down the barriers, Part 1: a question of space. *Hospital Development.* **24**(5).

8

The costs of rationalization

Introduction

The rationalization of acute care services will usually involve capital costs either for renovating facilities or building new ones. As such the NHS procedures of submitting an outline business case, and on approval of this a full business case, must be followed. Added to this procedure there is now the obligation to explore private finance under the private finance initiative (PFI).

While it is not the intention of this text to provide a detailed methodology for preparing an NHS business case, some key components of the process need to be described. In the final analysis the impact of rationalization on the costs of services becomes the all important concern. It is the primary objective of rationalization to use resources more effectively. In some instances, for example, where the new capitation formula has meant a reduction in funding, the aim of rationalization is to save funds in order to be able to deliver the same level of services with less money. In other instances the aim will be to make savings in order that substantial resources can be redeployed elsewhere, for example, in providing new services. Rationalization can never take place without a full analysis of the different options available for achieving the objectives, the potential savings, associated costs, and risk analysis. The aim of this chapter is to outline the areas which need to be taken into account in such an analysis.

Rationalization of services is not always associated with a reduction of beds; there are many opportunities for savings when beds are redistributed between sites, often resulting in site closure. A site closure results in a 100 per cent saving on estate cost and capital charges. Even reopening the same number of beds on an existing operational site will achieve substantial savings in the hotel services, management, and administration costs.

The analysis of options

Options analysis is the systematic examination of the different ways of meeting objectives before committing resources. It is important to think widely and creatively about the range of options before choosing a small number to appraise more fully.

In any situation it is usually possible to develop a list of six to eight options and then narrow them down to three or four feasible options for full analysis and costing. For example, in the case of North West Surrey Health Authority, three options were examined:

1   closing Ashford Hospital, Middlesex and redeveloping it as a community hospital

2   closing St Peter's Hospital, Chertsey and redeveloping it as a community hospital

3   keeping both sites as DGHs and achieving savings by a rationalization of services between the two sites.

In options analysis the first option is the 'do nothing' or 'do minimum' option, but even this option will have associated costs. Take, for example, the already cited case of Cardiff Royal Infirmary with the estimated need for a capital expenditure of £27.7 million to comply with statutory fire regulations. This cost would have to be included in the 'do nothing' option for acute care services in Cardiff.

The criteria by which the options are appraised will need to be determined in each individual case. When considering rationalizing acute care services the criteria used could include:

• quality of clinical care

• patient accessibility

• quality of the accommodation

• future flexibility

• acceptability to staff

• impact on education programmes.

Each of the criteria chosen needs to be weighted in order of importance so that the total of the weightings is 100. For each option the criteria are then scored between 1 and 10 and a sum of the criteria weights × score gives the total score of the option.

In developing the standard NHS business case it is recommended that the sensitivity of the options is examined by changing the weights given to each of the criteria and calculating the impact of this on the final score.

It is from these scores of the acceptability of the options to the chosen criteria that the highest scoring options should be selected for costing. It would normally be appropriate to cost out three or four options. The costing of options is time consuming and can require the buying in of costly services from architects and surveyors, etc., so the decision of how many options to cost cannot be taken lightly.

Costing the options

Costing the options includes the costs associated with achieving the desired options and their operating costs over a specified period. The guidance on developing the NHS business case for capital investments recommends that the specified period of appraisal should normally equate to the intended period of use of the building; for new hospital buildings this is conventionally assumed to be 60 years, and for existing buildings the remaining physical life of the building. In costing each option estimates will be required of:

- capital costs
- operating costs of running the trust
- opportunity costs of resources already owned
- consequential costs borne by others.

In addition, the costs and benefits of each option which cannot be quantified should be described in detail as they relate to the overall objectives of the project.

The cost of the 'do nothing' option forms the baseline for comparing the costs of all options. This cost will be the cost of extrapolating the present operating costs of the trust into the future on the assumption that the existing estate remains and is maintained in good condition.

Capital costs

The main elements which comprise capital costs are:

- land: the purchase price of new land or opportunity cost of land already owned
- works or building costs: these will usually be refurbishment and upgrading or construction of a new building, or a combination of both
- professional fees: associated with the planning, design, and execution of schemes and the purchase/disposal of property. It will include fees for architects, engineers, surveyors, project managers, and other professionals as required
- equipment: this will include new equipment, installation costs, and the value of transferred equipment.

Revenue costs

These are the actual costs associated with operating or running the service and will be based on assumptions of the volume of service to be provided and include:

- staff costs: i.e. medical, nursing, support services (pathology, pharmacy, therapies, etc.), and ancillary services (portering, security, etc.)

- management and administrative costs

- service costs: consumables and equipment maintenance

- estate costs: building maintenance, grounds maintenance, local authority business rates, utilities, rental/lease charges, and estate management

- contract services: catering, laundry, housekeeping.

Many trusts have already developed cost models linking service volumes to the main cost components of the service. With some adaptations these models can probably be used to project the running costs of various options. Computerized revenue/cost models, developed on spreadsheet software, can be combined with capital cost modules to produce cash flow projections, and from these discounted cash flows can be calculated. Capital charges and VAT (where applicable) should be subtracted from all costs before evaluating the discounted cash flows.

Discounted cash flow analysis

Discounted cash flow analysis is the technique used to compare options. This is a method of putting different options, which may have different time horizons and a different profile of capital and revenue cash flows, on to a common footing for comparison. This is done by converting all the future costs and revenues associated with each option to their equivalent value today (the net present value). The government applies a real discount rate of 6 per cent to all its projects, but the private sector will use a higher rate, because private sector companies can never raise capital as cheaply as the government.

Affordability of options

At this point the trust needs to assess the balance between options, weighing the net present value against the non-quantifiable aspects of the scheme, for example, environmental factors, questions of equity, planning feasibility.

Once the cash flows for each option have been calculated and set out the trust needs to consider two factors:

1   is the preferred option affordable?

2   what will be the impact of the options on the price to the purchasers?

In most instances a maximum capital expenditure will have been identified in terms of the funds likely to be available from one or a combination of possible sources. If the preferred option exceeds the capital ceiling it will be necessary to consider options for cost reduction. This could mean adopting a different design, altering the mix of new build, adaptation, renovation, or simply leaving some desired changes undone.

Any capital investment will result in increased depreciation charges and the need to realize a return on new assets which will be reflected in increased capital charges. In the case of the NHS, investments which increase operating costs, and hence the price to purchasers, will be difficult to justify. All new build carries a penalty in terms of higher capital charges because a new asset will have a higher value than an existing asset. However, depreciation will be spread over a longer period since the new asset will have a longer life than the existing asset.

Sensitivity to risk

In determining the costs and benefits of any option a number of assumptions will have been made. For example, operating costs will have been based on a defined level of patient activity or contracts placed; if this level is not achieved the actual revenue or income to the trust will be reduced, affecting the cash flow assumptions. Sensitivity analysis tests the robustness of the ranking of options. The most robust options are those which, even if the assumptions on which they are based turn out to be different, deliver the same benefits with the least variation in projected costs. It should be possible to analyse and measure the magnitude of the consequences of the risk and estimate the probability of the risk event occurring.

Risk arises from the possibility that more than one outcome can occur. A number of methods are available to analyse and quantify risk. Testing the sensitivity of options to variations in cost involves recalculating capital and revenue costs with various items set at different values, for example:

- labour costs could increase by a higher than anticipated amount due to government or trade union action

- cash receipts may not be achieved when expected, for example, if due to market conditions buildings or land cannot be sold, or is sold at a lower than planned price

- demand for services may be greater or lesser than planned

- the phasing of the project may change.

The aim should be to minimize the major risks. According to the nature of the project this can be achieved in a variety of ways. For example, the phasing of projects will often provide the flexibility for alteration if circumstances or methods of health care delivery change.

All major projects undertaken should have a risk management strategy. Such a strategy would:

- specify the key risks to the investment

- detail the 'early warning' indicators that will show that problems are arising

- provide a plan for monitoring the early warning indicators

- detail the action that will be taken to minimize the impact of changes.

The allocation of risk is a major factor in any large project. The governing premise of risk allocation is that the party best able to manage or control the risk should absorb the risk. The allocation of risk is a major issue in private finance initiative projects. A clear aim of PFI projects is to achieve optimum risk transfer.

The private finance initiative

The private finance initiative (PFI) was originally launched in 1992. The Department of Health's *Capital investment manual* (published in June 1994 to replace *Capricode guidance on NHS capital procurement*) makes it clear that all business cases for new capital investment in the NHS have to explore private finance.

As of February 1996, 46 PFI projects had been approved at an estimated value of £218 million. The first schemes to be approved tended to be small schemes valued at below £15 million, such as waste incinerators and staff accommodation. In 1995–96 some much larger schemes obtained approval; these include:

- South Buckinghamshire Trust: a £35 million new build/refurbishment scheme approved in November 1995. Includes an almost complete rebuild of Amersham General Hospital and an extra wing at Wycombe General Hospital. The private sector partner, Healthcare Group Consortium, will fund, design, and construct the new buildings on land leased from the trust. It will lease the buildings to the trust for a maximum of 60 years, after which the trust will take over ownership.

- St James' University Hospital Trust, Leeds: the second phase of a £50 million scheme was approved in January 1996. Private consortium Medipark (St James', Leeds) Ltd signed a development agreement in April 1995 to build a science park on land purchased from the trust. In phase two the consortium will build a new hospital wing on land leased from the trust. This will include 166 paediatric beds, an 80-bed private patients' unit, and a patients' hotel. The trust will sign an 80-year operational lease, with a break clause after 25 years.

In April 1996 two further major PFI projects were approved, a £90 million hospital replacement scheme at Swindon and Marlborough Trust and a £70 million Norfolk and Norwich Health Care Trust Hospital.

PFI in the NHS is still in its infancy and the 'rules' for many areas are still being written. Major criticisms so far are the length of time the PFI procurement takes, the policy of having to explore PFI for all capital projects when some are clearly not viable in the private sector, and the actual costs to both the trusts and the private sector of the planning process. According to some NHS sources a major advantage has been the innovative solutions put forward by the private sector in many cases. The major stages in the typical PFI process are outlined in Box 8.1.

Box 8.1: Major stages in the PFI process

1   Outline business case approval

2   Advertise in *The European Journal*

3   Expressions of interest received

4   Issue outline information

5   Select pre-qualified parties

6   Issue information memorandum

7   Receive price bids

8   Short-list bidders

9   Negotiations

10   Receive second stage bids

11   Evaluation process

12   Trust Board approval

13   Submission of full business case and PFI approval

Public relations, communications, and consultation

Introduction

In the process of rationalizing acute care beds good communications and public relations are essential both within the organization and externally. Everyone is familiar with newspaper and other media reports of beds being closed, hospitals being closed, and services discontinued. Such reports are usually negative, designed to develop a public outcry, and rarely attempt to explain in a clear and logical way the rationale behind the decisions. Aside from generating public opposition to the organization, such reports upset and demoralize staff who are worried about the security of their jobs. In these instances it is not wholly the media to blame for the negative presentation of the facts; managers must share the responsibility for failing to get their side of events to the general public and other concerned bodies.

The Audit Commission report, *Trusting in the future*, published in April 1994[1], identifies poor communication as one of the factors contributing to variable performance in NHS trusts. In 1994 the Office of Public Management undertook a survey on communications in the NHS involving all health authorities, FHSAs, health boards, and health commissions in the UK, and all first, second, and third wave trusts. Questionnaires were sent to chief executives of all these organizations and over a third responded. The Audit Commission report had stated that half of the trusts they investigated had a communication strategy. The Office of Public Management survey broadly supported this finding but found differences between internal and external strategies. Almost two-thirds of the trusts surveyed had an internal communications strategy, but just over half had an external strategy. While this supports the view that the importance of communications is being recognized, it is clear that in many organizations there is still a long way to go.

This chapter examines the importance of good communications and the role of public relations and public consultation in the rationalization of acute care services.

The role of public relations in hospitals

For at least the past two decades most hospitals in the USA have had a public relations department or at the least a public relations officer. The fact that the public relations function often reports directly to the Chief Executive or Deputy Chief Executive emphasizes the importance attributed to it.

With the introduction of the NHS in 1948, the general public were so enamoured with the services made available free of charge there was little need for much attention to be devoted to the hospital's public image. To a large extent this attitude has persisted up to the 1991 reforms. At this time the introduction of the internal market, competition, and the Patient's Charter brought home to most hospitals the need for good public relations.

The 1994 Office of Public Management report stressed the importance of 'high quality corporate communications to promote the service and motivate the workforce'. It also pointed out that communications staff, where they existed, were rarely linked to the senior management team.

Hospitals are now using a variety of public relations arrangements. Some have hired outside firms to prepare patient booklets and leaflets or have sometimes hired public relations consultants to handle particular issues. For example, in 1993 the then Lambeth, Southwark and Lewisham FHSA hired consultants to publicize primary health care developments being carried out as part of the Tomlinson recommendations. The FHSA was pleased with the publicity and interest generated in the media and felt the consulting firm hired had good contacts with the media which they themselves could not have developed over the short term.

More recently there is a growing trend for larger hospitals to recruit in-house public relations or communications officers. There is also the disturbing trend of hospitals appointing in-house managers, whose jobs are no longer required, into the public relations role. While such persons may have years of NHS experience and a good understanding of the organization and its goals, public relations is a profession in its own right and not a set of skills that can be acquired overnight or by attending a few seminars. There are many professionals, especially clinicians, who will view the appointment of public relations managers as more money being directed away from patient care. It is the task of senior managers to address this issue and convert the disbelievers. This can never be achieved if the public relations team is not delivering visible results, and good results will not be delivered by amateurs.

It is not the intent of this chapter to review in detail the functions of public relations, but to concentrate on those attributes which are essential to the process of acute care services rationalization. Any organization considering a major rationalization programme should consider creating an in-house public relations function if one does not already exist or hiring the services of a public relations consultant. In an exercise of this nature senior managers will have additional demands on their time and will not have sufficient time or expertise to handle all the necessary public relations functions.

The public relations function should always be proactive and not reactive. An in-house director of public relations must establish good relationships with the local media. They can do a lot to promote a good image of the hospital in the community by regularly feeding the media with reports of new services or developments. With or without an in-house public relations function the hospital Chief Executive should make sure he knows the editor of the local paper and seek ways of involving him in any major hospital events or functions. In these ways when negative events do take place the channels of communication are already open for the hospital to present its side of the story.

As soon as planning for rationalization commences a press release should be prepared to inform the media on the process, the rationale for undertaking it, and the expected time of any outcomes. Once the plan is fully developed a press conference should be held to outline the plan, give the media representatives a written summary of the plan, and the Chief Executive should be present to answer any questions and concerns. Most media reporters have busy jobs and will tend to use verbatim large chunks of any well prepared press release in their articles. This saves them a lot of time, guarantees they get the facts correct, and helps them out in situations where they may be having difficulty in fully comprehending the issues involved.

At the same time there should be a well-developed programme for senior managers to use every opportunity to go out and personally present the plan to concerned groups. Such groups would include the local medical society, the community health councils, voluntary associations, etc. All local GPs should be sent a special communication outlining the plan and addressing what are known or expected to be their concerns. If these actions are carried out effectively there is no reason for negative or sensational reporting of the planned events.

The public consultation process which must accompany any rationalization exercises should not be seen as a substitute for public relations. Consultation processes are usually quite limited in the number of people reached, so even if consensus is obtained the general public are usually left ignorant of events until they see or hear it through the local media.

Internal communications

The importance of good internal communications throughout any rationalization process cannot be emphasized too strongly; in some ways it is even more essential than the external communications and public relations exercises. In many instances hospitals are the largest employer in the area and most of the staff will have local families, friends, and neighbours with whom they relate on a regular basis. If the staff are well informed, understand what is taking place, and support the changes, a positive message can be transmitted through them to a large part of the local community.

The method by which good internal communications are achieved will depend on the organization. Some hospitals have in place systems for achieving effective internal communications. Before any process of rationalization commences the effectiveness of existing communications systems should be reviewed or a system developed to keep staff at all levels informed. Again, verbal messages can be misunderstood or misheard; a written communication can be kept and reread or referred to for clarification at a later time. Whatever method is adopted the process of communications should be two-way, with a means for staff to express their concerns and these concerns to be handled in a timely fashion.

Any internal communications process must also involve the voluntary groups which work within the hospital; they not only devote a lot of time and provide a valuable service but are often influential in the local community.

Openness and clarity

No matter how good the systems for internal and external communications are they will fail if the message is not clear, honest and readily understood. The use of NHS 'jargon', abstract concepts, and unfamiliar terms can be confusing, both to NHS staff and to the general public.

It has to be borne in mind that many employees within the organization, both unskilled and professional, will have less than a clear picture of the structure of the organization and how it actually functions. The majority of the general public will have even less idea. Therefore on both fronts a lot of time and expertize will have to be used in developing the message.

Another key issue is credibility and confidence in the management. Sometimes it may be necessary to be more open and give out more information, particularly about aims and objectives, than senior managers feel comfortable with in the so-called competitive environment. Credibility will not be achieved either internally or externally if the recipients of the message feel they are not getting the full story.

In some instances openness and clarity will involve sharing information which is unfavourable to the hospital and some issues will be more emotive than others. A good example of this is anything to do with paediatric beds. In recent years a number of smaller hospitals have had to close the few paediatric beds they had as an acceptable level of quality paediatric care could not be delivered on such a small scale. They could neither afford nor attract qualified paediatric specialist staff. Many of these decisions have caused a public outcry, in most cases because the real reason for the closure was not articulated. It takes a brave manager to stand up and tell his local community that the care his organization is providing in a certain specialty is not up to scratch and that he would not like his own family to be treated there. However, armed with this information most parents would happily take their children another five miles down the road to a well staffed, high quality paediatric department.

The public consultation process

Alongside the public relations role is the statutory requirement for public consultation when changes in services are being planned. The Community Health Council (Amendment) Regulations 1990 – which take into account the NHS and Community Care Act – make purchasers responsible for consulting about the detailed service proposals of trusts.

There is considerable confusion at the national level and an urgent need to redefine the consultation responsibilities of purchasers and providers. This confusion should not be used by providers as a means to opt out of consultation and leave the responsibility to the purchaser. The provider may be going through a major change in service provision, for example, reducing beds or closing a site, which has been driven or encouraged by the purchaser; however, this is no reason to leave the public consultation process to the purchaser alone. This is another instance where good public relations strategy and advice in-house can be invaluable. At the very least the provider should take joint responsibility with the purchaser for the public consultation. This will involve both writing the consultation documents (as the provider is in a much better position to describe their own services than the purchaser is) and agreeing the process, which groups to consult, and how to go about it.

As discussed in other parts of this book, there is now fairly widespread professional agreement on the future organization of the NHS in terms of the future size of general hospitals, the requirements for A&E departments, staffing levels needed to improve junior doctors' hours, and the need for fewer but larger tertiary centres. The wide range of reasons for rationalizing acute care services have been discussed in detail. However, as soon as anything smacking of reducing beds or closing sites gets into the public domain the media tends to provide a very negative slant on the story. The tendency to equate quality with quantity is paramount. A more open and public relations-led consultation process by the providers themselves can do much to increase public understanding and gain public support.

In support of the importance of good internal communications and consultation prior to going outside of the organization is the lesson to be learned from the opposition to plans to reconfigure London's acute care services. Much of this opposition was led by the staff of the hospitals themselves. They attracted national media attention in a way that would have been a credit to some of the country's leading public relations firms and mobilized their patients and their families into what amounted to a crusade. If this energy and the intimate knowledge that only the front line staff have of the services they deliver, their strengths, and their weaknesses, could have been redirected into a less emotional and more rational approach the future acute care services of the capital would be second to none.

The need for less but better consultation

The two studies by Jill Turner published by the IHSM, *Current issues in acute care: reconfiguring acute services*[2] and *Current issues in acute care: reconfiguring acute services II*[3] illustrate how public protest is thwarting a threatened wave of hospital closures across the UK. For example, in Bristol, Surrey, and Birmingham, health authority proposals to close an acute hospital, or remove its acute services, have been dropped in favour of less unpopular means of saving cash. In many other cases public protest has delayed and frustrated the timely implementation of plans.

Recently there have been numerous published articles on how best to go about the public consultation process; to some degree the whole process seems to be getting out of hand. Many health authorities are spending inordinate amounts of time and money on the process and frequently ending up having to change well thought out and appropriate plans prepared by experts to accommodate the often emotional and ill-informed views of the general public. The fact that most responses received in any consultation exercise are negative must not be lost sight of; people in support of proposals generally do not bother to send in their positive responses. Just because a vociferous minority object is no reason to change plans if they can be proved to result in better and more effective health care; if they cannot prove this they were not well developed in the first place and must be changed. Money spent on public consultation is money which is not being used for direct patient care; an example of this is presented in Box 9.1.

Box 9.1: Example of public consultation

Lambeth, Southwark and Lewisham Health Authority consulted on proposals for changes to acute care services at Guy's Hospital and St Thomas' Hospital.

During the consultation over 10 000 consultation documents and 150 000 summaries were distributed and 50 meetings were held. The direct cost to the commission was over £70 000 with staff costs probably twice as much again.

After consultation, the main strategic decision was confirmed, but commitments were strengthened to develop other services in the area. Also the closure of Guy's A&E was delayed until 1999 at the earliest.

This is not to say that consultation *per se* is a total waste of time and money. Any consultation exercise must distinguish between consultation with 'stakeholders' and consultation with the general public. Stakeholders include purchasers, providers, GPs, and GPFHs, local authorities, community health councils, and a large number of voluntary organizations which represent the interests of specific patient groups. These groups must be included in the early stages of the planning process. In many respects if this is done correctly the views of the service users should have been well represented, taken into account, and can only enhance the final outcome.

The confusion between consultation and patient involvement

It is now time for the NHS Executive to think more clearly about appropriate levels of public and patient involvement in our health care system.

In 1992 the NHS Executive published *Local voices: the views of local people in purchasing for health*. The main recommendations of this document were:

- health authorities were urged to seek a representative cross section of local views

- the advantage of getting the public on board was that 'As health authorities seek to bring about changes in services and make explicit decisions about priorities, they are more likely to be successful in their negotiations with providers if they secure public support'

- a combination of techniques for involving the public was recommended with a warning about 'over-reliance on any one method'

- the techniques recommended included: public meetings; local voluntary groups; health forums; rapid appraisal; community initiatives; telephone hotlines; surveys of public opinion; patient satisfaction surveys; one-to-one interviews; complaints procedures.

Most people would agree that even four years after the publication of *Local voices* public participation in service planning remains patchy. The *Priorities and planning guidance for 1996–97* also lists national priorities in the medium term as 'giving greater influence to users of NHS services and their carers'.

The National Association of Health Authorities and Trusts in its paper *Reshaping the NHS*, published in June 1995, looked at a sample of 66 out of 108 health authority plans, and concluded that much was said about involving the public but little was actually achieved.

One means health authorities seem to be favouring is establishing large standing panels of citizens and surveying them periodically on a range of issues; in some instances they have provided funds to the community health councils (CHCs) to carry out such surveys. In other areas where the health authorities take on these tasks themselves one has to question if the CHCs have much of a role left any more. Maybe what is needed is a more appropriate level of funding to the CHCs, so they can do what they were established to do in the first place, namely, 'represent the interests in the health service of the public in their district'.

It would be interesting to see how many private industries could survive in a competitive market if every time they wanted to make a change in the level and type of goods produced or services offered they had to go out and consult with the general public and be guided by their views. The basis of competition is to satisfy the consumer by offering goods and services at a level and quality acceptable to them; if this is not done the business will not survive and neither will NHS trusts. The time has come to give NHS managers and planners some credit for understanding their professions and to let them get on with providing the best possible services within the limited resources available, without having to play this charade of public consultation every time they want to change something.

The private industry sector spends a lot of funds on market research in order to ensure that its goods and services are acceptable to the consumers. While not having the same level of budget available, managers on both the provider and purchaser sides will welcome the chance to consult with patients and their families on the services they receive, their satisfaction with such services, and suggestions for change. The information from this process is a valuable addition to improving services.

References

1   The Audit Commission. (1994) *Trusting in the future*. HMSO.

2   Turner J. (1994) *Current issues in acute care: reconfiguring acute services*. IHSM.

3   Turner J. (1995) *Current issues in acute care: reconfiguring acute services II*. IHSM.

10

Future uncertainties

Introduction

Although only four years away there is no precise blueprint for the NHS in the 21st century, indeed at the present time there are many uncertainties. One of the greatest uncertainties will be the general election in 1997 or sooner. The change from a Conservative government to a Labour or Liberal Democrat-led country will bring significant changes to the structure and functioning of the NHS. Both opposition parties have produced health policies and these are examined in this chapter.

The future, regardless of a change in government, will require further structural changes to cope with the needs of improving clinical effectiveness and more emphasis on directing resources to services and procedures with proven outcomes. Achieving the necessary integration between primary, secondary, and tertiary care still has a long way to go. The issue of rationing care and establishing priorities is now much in the public debate and will continue to be developed and evolve.

Health service managers cannot sit back and wait for these changes to occur; they must now be establishing their positions through vision and strategic thinking in order that the work of their organizations will not be jeopardized by external events.

Alternative health policies

The Labour Party health policy

The Labour Party released its health policy document, *Renewing the NHS*, at the end of June 1995. This followed the launch 18 months prior to this of its consultation document, *Health 2000*. At the launch of *Renewing the NHS* the Labour leader Tony Blair made the following statement:

> It is preserving the best of what is there, but changing the worst – and that is what we call the third way. It is a sensible way through, with what has been good about

the changes made – namely the devolution of greater control and power and the separation between planning and delivery – and the removal of what has been bad, which is this competitive market system and massive transaction costs.

Renewing the NHS identifies five priorities for the NHS which will underlie all Labour's plans for the health service; these are:

- tackling health inequalities

- improving general practice

- extending informed patient choice

- developing services based on research and evaluation of success rates, rather than just speed of treatment

- providing a rational and fair framework of services for elderly people.

The major changes a Labour government would make to the current system are:

- abolish the internal market

- return trust hospital assets to public ownership

- phase out GP fundholding and replace it with GP commissioning

- all GPs will be able to refer patients to the consultant or hospital of their choice

- health authorities and GPs will commission health care from hospitals

- abolish the income tax relief on health insurance for the over 60s

- review of paybeds and private practice in the NHS

- establish a royal commission on long-term care

- put local representatives on the boards of health authorities and trusts

- give more power to CHCs

- appoint a minister for public health.

A recurring theme in the document is the intent to create more patient and consumer groups. Local people will have a much greater say in the planning of services and monitoring standards. There is also a lot of emphasis on accountability, especially at the local level, but without any clear indication of what it is. There is a commitment to end compulsory competitive tendering.

Basically health authorities and trusts would be reintegrated, but trusts would be allowed to continue having day-to-day managerial independence. Annual contracting will be replaced by long-term comprehensive health care agreements. Without sufficient detail in the policy document it is difficult to see how the concept of all GPs being free to refer where they wish fits with the idea of budgeted comprehensive health care agreements. After consultation with health professionals, new standards will be set for service quality, clinical effectiveness, and managerial performance.

The document leaves a couple of key areas in limbo; the fate of the regional tier and its functions and the private finance initiative. Labour had indicated a need for a strategic regional presence but made no commitment one way or another to the private finance initiative. As a Labour government would be faced with between £600 million and £700 million of projects in the pipeline, it is unlikely to be able to scrap it and look to the Treasury for the funds. In a statement issued in July 1996, the shadow health secretary, Harriet Harman, said that a Labour government would 'direct and control' the use of private finance in the NHS by setting national and regional priorities for capital development and using private finance within a 'public sector-led planning framework'.

In the final analysis it is not at all clear what impact these proposed changes will have on the day-to-day running of acute care trusts. No doubt some of the proposals will be welcomed as saving substantial time and resources, namely, the move away from annual contracts into longer-term agreements and the move away from compulsory competitive tendering. What still remains very much in the dark is the balance of power between the purchasers and the providers. If trusts are to be accountable again to health authorities, the situation where the health authority has a vested interest in contracting with its own provider will be paramount; the question then becomes how to rein in the GPs who supposedly will have freedom of referral.

In June 1996, just a year after the Labour Party issued it's health policy document, Tony Blair, addressing a meeting of the National Association of Health Authorities and Trusts, appeared to be modifying some of Labour's proposed changes. He said that the distinction between purchasers and providers would remain and made it very clear that Labour would not repeat the pledge made at the last general election to restore underfunding in the NHS. The first task would be to look at whether money was being well spent and treatments were effective: 'Only after these two stages have been gone through would a Labour government look at whether there was still a funding gap that needed to be bridged'.

The uncertainty over what Labour intends to do about fundholding GPs remains. The aim, it seems, is to give all GPs an equal say in shaping hospital services for their patients. He stated that Labour would not make political appointments to trust and health authority boards, but would follow the Nolan Committee's recommendations that appointments should be made on merit. The only new announcement was that Labour would set up a task force to try to end the practice of patients having to spend hours on trolleys in hospital emergency departments.

As a general election gets closer, more refinements or changes to the proposed policies can be expected. Establishing task forces and taking on nebulous tasks such as trying to ascertain the effectiveness of different treatments are at best well intentioned, but at the same time expensive and long-term projects which may be seen by some as stalling tactics.

The Liberal Democrat health policy

Building on the best of the NHS outlines the Liberal Democrat health policy. This policy would:

- maintain the purchaser–provider division

- increase the contracting cycle and require trusts to publish their pricing policy and introduce quality and standard indicators

- establish a national inspectorate of health and social services to assess, investigate, and monitor standards in public and private healthcare

- boost local accountability on trust boards, health authorities, and through CHCs by including on them more elected members of relevant local authorities

- GP fundholding will not be abolished, but it is expected to fade out in favour of local commissioning groups

- all GPs will be required to participate in local health planning and consultation with other major health organizations

- all health needs will be met through a centrally funded NHS

- tobacco tax will be increased to provide increased funds for the NHS

- in view of the fact that the NHS can never provide all services immediately, continuing assessment of rationing and priority setting procedures will be an essential part of the strategy.

Again the policy is very lacking in detail, but the message is clear; no major structural changes but an increased emphasis on quality, standards, and local accountability.

The private sector

It is not clear what a Labour government would do about NHS pay-beds, although it would be harder than it was in the Barbara Castle era to eliminate them. There are now more of them and they are a major income source for many trusts. The 1995 *Fitzhugh directory on private health care* estimates that £115 million was generated by the NHS from private patient work, representing a growing share of a growing market; other sources put the amount at closer to £200 million. Three London trusts, the Royal Free, Guy's and St Thomas', and University College Hospital generated over £8 million each from private care and a further 10 trusts earn more than £2 million a year in pay-bed revenue. For each of the top 10, private patient revenue amounts to more than 2 per cent of income; in the case of Harefield Hospital and the Nuffield Orthopaedic Centre it accounts for more than 10 per cent.

In May 1996, the health insurance company BUPA stunned NHS trusts by establishing a new health fund in which subscribers will have to be treated at designated private hospitals rather than in an NHS private unit. The BUPA plan involves 148 hospitals in total and includes the BUPA hospitals, BMI hospitals, and Nuffield hospitals. By guaranteeing a high level of occupancy BUPA has been able to negotiate a 20 per cent discount. The subscribers to the fund have been offered financial benefits worth 8 per cent of their subscriptions. BUPA claimed that the prospect of a Labour government and subsequent instability of pay-beds was a factor in the decision to exclude NHS hospitals. BUPA also claimed that treatment costs in the NHS have risen faster than in other hospitals. BUPA patients would still be permitted to use NHS hospitals if the treatment they required was not available in the private sector.

Clearly this came as a shock to NHS managers and it is the kind of move that is very difficult to anticipate. BUPA holds about 45 per cent of the private health insurance policies. Before the other major insurers follow this lead, NHS pay-bed managers need to closely examine their cost structures and also review their case mix to see what portion of their private business comprises specialized procedures not normally undertaken in the private sector.

Priorities and rationing

Establishing priorities and rationing services are issues which are very much in the forefront of health care spending and likely to remain there for the foreseeable future. These issues are not new to the NHS; resources have always been finite and such decisions have been made through waiting lists and the level of services provided. The difference now is that the debate is much more in the public arena and both health authorities and clinicians are increasingly willing to publicize their decisions.

In 1974 an American professor of economics and community medicine, Dr Victor Fuchs, authored a book entitled *Who shall live: health economics and social choice*.[1] Although based on the American health care service at that time, his findings and recommendations are as relevant today as they were over 22 years ago. He concludes that:

- increased spending on health care is not in direct relationship to increased good health

- health has less to do with what we spend on health care then our heredity, environment, and personal lifestyles

- decisions by physicians with respect to hospitalization, surgery, prescriptions, and tests largely determine what is spent on health care

- we can never have for everyone all the health and medical care we would like, therefore choices have to be made.

At this time and in the American context his recommendations called for:

- universal comprehensive health insurance

- decentralized and locally delivered care with tertiary care delivered at the regional level

- competition amongst providers

- greater use of physician extenders

- a regulated and rational supply of physicians between the specialties in relation to need

- rational hospital utilization, pointing to the dangers and costs of over-bedding.

In September 1995 the forum on *Healthcare 2000*, led by Sir Duncan Nichol, issued its report. Among its conclusions the report stated that it had found no conclusive evidence that the NHS was under-funded but went on to say '. . . but there is a gap between resources and demand which shows signs of increasing as we move into the next century'. It then goes on to say that it sees some form of rationing as inevitable.

At the present time it is the policy of the government that priority setting has to be carried out at the local level. Health authorities are already making some explicit 'rationing' type decisions. Berkshire Health Authority has banned three procedures for 1996–97, labelling them as 'non-essential'; these are abdominoplasty, sex changes, and removal of wisdom teeth. The action was taken to help clear a £7 million deficit. The treatments will still be available if there is a clear clinical need. The health authority already refuses to fund some other procedures including in-vitro fertilization, reversal of sterilization, cosmetic surgery, and alternative therapies on the NHS. A NAHAT survey of 66 health authority purchasing plans for 1994–95 showed 11 rationing explicitly compared to four in the previous year. In some respects the Patient's Charter and its emphasis on waiting times has forced rationing out into the public domain. Prior to this, consultants could keep minor cases which they felt to be 'non-essential' or very low in priority at the bottom of their waiting lists for years.

There is a question of semantics here in that many of the services being so-called 'rationed' are those which evidence has indicated give no patient benefit; for example, removal of grommets, and D&Cs. Eradicating such procedures should not be described as rationing as much as making more effective use of resources.

Evidence-based medicine

A major problem in health care which has always been with us and is likely to remain is the evaluation of the effectiveness of different treatments. This is now popularly known as evidence-based medicine or EBM. EBM has been defined as 'the process of systematically finding, appraising, and using contemporaneous research findings as the basis for clinical decisions'. At the present time EBM is central to health policy. Purchasers are universally talking in terms of evidence-based purchasing (EBP).

There is a *Journal of Evidence Based Medicine* and the *Effective Health Care* bulletins produced by Leeds University and York University provide evidence of the effectiveness of selected interventions. The bulletins, which are circulated to all provider and purchasing units, are based on a systematic review and synthesis of published research. Central government support for this approach is illustrated by the NHS research and development programme and major investment in academic centres such as the Cochrane Centre and the NHS Centre for Reviews and Dissemination.

Very few people would argue against the concept of EBM. In the present climate the danger is that it is being acclaimed as the panacea for all the problems associated with limited resources. The idea is that all problems will be resolved if purchasing can be based on the evidence of the efficacy of the different treatment regimes available. In reality this is not going to occur as the complexity of many conditions does not lend itself to such straightforward analysis. While purchasers may refuse to fund some specific procedures or develop protocols for treating certain conditions the NHS will not survive if the clinicians themselves are not permitted to exercise their professional judgement on behalf of their patients. The emphasis of EBM must be to make the findings readily available to the clinicians involved in front line patient care rather than to the budget holders.

The fact that the emphasis is on devolving the establishing of priorities down to local levels means that while one health commission may choose to fund a certain procedure its next-door neighbour may not; this presents a major dilemma for both the clinicians and patients involved.

From the perspective of the health service manager this is another area of uncertainty which has to be considered in the planning of service provision. It means that the clinicians involved in each specialty have to be relied upon to closely monitor the EBM developments in their specialties, and to keep general management informed of potential changes which could occur if the primary purchasers decided to withdraw funding for common procedures which are suddenly being questioned, and may be provisioned for, in the planning of bed requirements, theatre time, and staffing levels.

The era of cooperation between competing providers

In the initial stages of the NHS reforms and the competitiveness created by the internal market forces, the idea of actually cooperating or entering into agreements with competing trusts was an enigma to most managers. However, the evidence that this may be the way of the future is beginning to emerge. Many trusts are entering into agreements with other trusts to provide or share specific clinical services. A substantial amount of this cooperation is driven by staffing shortages, primarily medical staff, and in other instances when a trust does not have a sufficient volume of business to meet the minimum standards for certain procedures.

A recent NAHAT survey[2] indicated that 79 per cent of the 174 trusts responding were having problems recruiting consultants and other non-training grades. Problems ranged from no response to advertisements to a very poor field of candidates. In training grades 146 trusts (83 per cent) reported recruitment problems mainly at the senior house officer and registrar levels. Psychiatry, paediatrics, and A&E were the specialties with the greatest problems.

Trade-offs are beginning to emerge where trusts agree to divide the work in certain specialties, one doing a certain set of procedures and the other doing a different set of procedures within the same specialty. The sharing of clinical services is probably just the tip of the iceberg; there are many non-clinical services which lend themselves to this type of arrangement. Even in the very competitive hospital arena in the US this type of cooperation has existed for many years. Hospitals in the same area often form consortia for sharing non-clinical services and it is quite common to enter into clinical service agreements where one hospital will agree not to provide a certain service provided by a competitor and the competitor in return agrees not to provide a different service. Many of these agreements are in areas involving major capital expenditures where if the hospital down the road offers the same service there is not enough business for both hospitals to recoup their capital costs. The US experience has shown that once the foundation for cooperation has been established it will continue to grow.

This is a good way forward for UK hospitals in the future and it supports the hub and spoke concept. In reality there is more than enough business to go around; the concentration has to be on structuring the service to deliver high-quality care in the most cost-effective way.

Conclusion

The whole issue of rationalization is concerned with making the most effective use of the resources available. At the current stage of evolution of the UK health care system rationalization in the acute care sector is primarily concerned with closing sites, closing beds, moving beds between services, and moving beds from one site to another. In most instances it has been forced upon the providers concerned as the only means available to continue to provide the levels and quality of services required without any increases in funding. While the process is long and tedious and often controversial it is providing opportunities to revise and update services, and in many instances to upgrade or replace outdated facilities.

This text has attempted to describe the reasons behind rationalization, provide an outline of the process involved, and discuss some of the issues which will impact on the future organization and structure of acute care in the NHS. There are many uncertainties in the immediate future even without contemplating a change in government. No one fully understands the total impact of a primary care-led NHS, or if it is achievable. Care in the community is a wonderful concept but still has a long way to go, and some aspects could prove too expensive. Once rationalization of the acute care sector has been achieved and the other efficiency measures such as increases in day cases and reductions in length of stay have peaked, where will the next opportunities to save resources come from? To some degree the next course is already being started with the moves towards more explicit rationing, evidence-based medicine, and cooperation alongside competition.

Life in the acute care sector has always had its excitement and challenges; these will surely increase. In this environment hospital managers must be prepared to lead and not wait to be led; they must be proactive and not just reactive. Above all they should ensure that they, and not the health authority or the general public, are running their own hospital. They must learn not to be cajoled into buying into the latest trends in health care or management if such concepts do not seem of any benefit to their organization. They must negotiate with purchasers and the regional offices from a position of strength gained through information and a clear direction of where their organization is going in the future. They should not be afraid to cooperate with the 'competition'. The tools for surviving and prospering in this uncertain climate of the future are information, good communications, and strategic thinking.

References

1   Fuchs V. (1974) *Who shall live: health economics and social change.* Basic Books, Inc.

2   NAHAT (1996) *Hospital and community health medical recruitment survey 1996.*

Index